A WRITER'S YEAR

By Fennel Hudson:

A MEANINGFUL LIFE
A WATERSIDE YEAR
A WRITER'S YEAR
WILD CARP
FLY FISHING
TRADITIONAL ANGLING
THE QUIET FIELDS
FINE THINGS
A GARDENER'S YEAR
THE LIGHTER SIDE
FRIENDSHIP
NATURE ESCAPE
BOOK OF SECRETS
THE PURSUIT OF LIFE

Fennel's Journal

No. 3

A WRITER'S YEAR

By

Fennel Hudson

2017
FENNEL'S PRIORY LIMITED

Published by Fennel's Priory Limited

www.fennelspriory.com

First shared as handwritten letters in 2008
Limited edition magazine published in 2012
Abridged eBook published in 2013
This extended edition published in 2017

Copyright © Fennel Hudson 2008, 2017

Fennel Hudson has asserted his right under the
Copyright, Designs and Patents Act 1988
to be identified as the author of this work.

All rights reserved. No part of this publication may be
reproduced, stored in a retrieval system or transmitted,
in any form or by any means, electronic, mechanical,
photocopying, recording or otherwise, without
the prior permission of Fennel's Priory Limited.

"Stop – Unplug – Escape – Enjoy"
and The Priory Flower logo are registered trademarks.

A CIP catalogue record for this book
is available from the British Library.

ISBN 978-1-909947-10-8

Available to purchase in other formats
at www.fennelspriory.com

Designed and typeset in 12pt Adobe Garamond Premier Pro.
Produced in England by Fennel's Priory Limited.

DEDICATIONS

To Liz Levey
for being the English teacher whose guidance,
enthusiasm and patience instilled my
lifelong love of language.

To Peter Wheat
for being my inspiration and counsel,
and for helping me to understand that absolute
focus is a talent that should be focused absolutely
on that which matters. Writing may be my
lifeblood, but family is everything.

And to the memory of Muriel Telford
whose softly-spoken voice echoes in my mind
every time I pick up a book. The time she spent
with me as a child, reading stories that fuelled
my imagination, was the greatest gift of all.

CONTENTS

Introduction 1
Measures of Success 5
A Room Full of Books 33
To be an Author 43
From Me to You 49
Handwritten Letters 55
His Nibs 63
The Magic Within 71
A New Writing Desk 79
Type, Writer 83
Out and About With a Notebook 89
Candlelight 95
Making an Impression 101
The Night Shift 107
'Dictionery' 113
Away From It All 119
Writing in Church 123
The Creative Fire 133
The Lost Story of a Lost Pen 137
The Golden Rules of Writing 141
Look Back, but Never Look Down 151

About the Author 153
The Fennel's Journal Series 157

STOP – UNPLUG – ESCAPE – ENJOY

This book, and the series to which it belongs, is about freedom. It's also about the adventures to be had when pursuing one's dreams, developing and communicating one's self, and striving for a slow-paced rural life. It's your opportunity to take time out from the stresses of modern living, to stop the wheels for a while, unplug from the daily grind, escape to a quiet and peaceful place, to enjoy the simple life. Because of this, I'd like you to read it in a distraction-free and relaxing environment: your 'safe place' where you can savour quality time and, if possible, delight in the beauty of the countryside.

That's why the book is pocket-sized, has a waxy cover and is printed using a special waterproof ink. It's designed to be taken with you on your travels. Don't store it in pristine condition upon a bookshelf; allow it to reflect the adventures you've had. Use a leaf as a bookmark and annotate the pages in the spaces provided with ideas of how you will honour your right to 'never do anything that offends your soul'.

The more mud-splattered, grass-stained, and pencil-scribbled this book becomes, the more you've demonstrated your ability to pursue a contented country life. So go on: live your life, be authentic, and always remember to 'Stop – Unplug – Escape – Enjoy'.

fennel

"The two most engaging powers of an author are to make new things familiar, and familiar things new."

Samuel Johnson

FULL STOP

A quick word before we begin. I have an urgent message that needs to be said. So listen up. I want you to write more letters. On paper. And with a proper pen. Then post them to your friends. It's not difficult. So no excuses. Don't think that you can't write. Because you can. Put pen to paper. Write. You don't even need neat handwriting. Or have much to say. "Hello" is enough. Your friends will appreciate the gesture. So write. Make the effort.

Start simply. Vocabulary and punctuation might bring one's writing to life. But they're only marks upon the page. Not all of them are necessary. You can get by with less than you think. Words like discombobulate can be discombobulating if used too frequently alongside other words that make us uneasy or confused. Like mytacism. Mmmm. I say again. Mmmm. And hardly anyone uses punctuation marks like the irony mark or the interrobang. How ironic that such questionable exclamation is barely used these days. Leave the advanced stuff until later. Begin with simple words and use just one punctuation mark. Like I'm doing here. Punctuating with full stops. Nothing more.

You don't need to be a skilled wordsmith to write letters. Just wear your heart on your sleeve. Write about what you think and feel. And share it with your friends.

There. I've made my point. Period.

INTRODUCTION

Writing: it's the gift of expression. Being able to capture one's thoughts and communicate with others is a privilege that we writers enjoy. But the old-school way of writing, with pen and ink, is a dying art. The writer's tool has progressed beyond the fountain pen and typewriter. Today we have a word processor within our laptop or desktop computer – even within our mobile phone. We can tap away onto a keyboard or, as is often done by journalists, speak into dictation software that converts our words into text. If we can think it, we can write it. Or should I say 'speak it'?

Writing is a form of communication. Its success lies in the strength and clarity of our message and its ability to be heard and understood by our reader. It's about choosing what to say and sharing it in a way that inspires someone. But, as Bob Dylan sang, "The times, they are a-changin'". We writers should "keep our eyes wide…and not speak too soon". Well, while times are a-changin', there's something I need to say: communication should be personal, intimate and as 'one-to-one' as possible. It should resonate and have meaning. Which, in this book, means talking slowly and clearly. It might help if you read it slowly too. I want you to imagine looking into my eyes when I speak, as there's more communicated in what we *don't* say than what we do. The deepest messages are to be found in the silence between words. Do you hear?

Today's cacophony of tweets and online chatter makes it harder for us to listen clearly. Attitudes to communication, and the technology that 'enables' it, have changed. We live in an age when, it seems, anything that isn't electrical is deemed artificial. Children can sit in the same room, looking at a television screen, playing a computer game where two children are sitting in the same room, talking to each other. A tennis racket is now a four-inch bar of white plastic and a five-year-old can drive a Formula 1 car. Well, I have a response to that: the Royal 'Wii' is not amused.

It must be a sign of my approaching middle age, but I find the modern entertainment culture to be completely alien to the natural and organic world that I know and love. When I was a boy (I'm sounding old now, even though I'm only 34) much enjoyment could be had dropping sycamore seeds from an upstairs window, or playing conkers, digging holes, or climbing trees. The world was there to be explored. Now there is an electronic curtain pulled across all that is real. Birdsong is muffled and replaced with the 'surround sound' of a virtual world of computer games where people can die and be reborn within a weekend. No wonder it's the new religion.

Progress isn't always good and there's a reason why 'breakneck speed' is described as such. A bullet travels quickly, but usually comes to an abrupt and fatal end. It's

INTRODUCTION

better to explore the slow lane, where we can properly see, hear and feel the beauty of the world; where words, carefully considered and understood, reveal truths that might otherwise be missed.

One thing that has apparently come to an end is the thoughtful and careful art of handwriting. If the fax machine didn't kill it then email sure did. Schoolchildren as young as six are given laptop computers upon which they learn to type. "How is your handwriting?" I ask. "Do you write in pencil or pen?" And, critically importantly, "Have you mastered the correct way to hold your writing implement?" They stare back at me with squinting eyes and a look that needs no words: *get with it grandad.*

In 1988, when I was at school, we still had exercise books and wrote using fountain pens. Nobody knew of laptop computers and Biro's were only used as impromptu blowpipes. There were no mobile phones in school and no lunchtime 'chat rooms'. Instead, pupils would play outdoors or read indoors. I would usually be found in the library, reading as much as I could to free my mind and inspire my soul. I wrote my first book during this time, a short fantasy novel about mystical beings that inhabited a subterranean world. The school published it for their *Dungeons & Dragons* club and it earned me a place at The Sorcerers' Table in the school canteen. Why do I mention this? Well, exactly twenty years later, I find myself penning this book. There are no mystical creatures here, no wizards or elves, but what compels me to write now is the same as all those years ago. It is the love of writing and storytelling, driven by a desire to escape. 'Not from, but to' a place of meaning.

Writing onto real paper, using a fountain pen and ink from a bottle, is the simplest of things. Yet it can transport us to a different place and time. Imagination is the real magic that exists in this world. Look inwards, to see outwards, and capture it in writing.

Bonus Chapter 2017

I

MEASURES OF SUCCESS

You're a writer. You feel it in your heart. But you don't know it yet. Your head is too busy thinking of ways to earn money. And why wouldn't it? You're ten years old and doing your best to survive in a capitalist world. That *Star Wars* figure won't pay for itself, y'know.

Something has to be done. So you look within – for talents that might set you free. You're great at listening and empathising. You're patient and kind. You relate to people and see the relationships between things. You have an eye for detail, an ability to observe. You can see – and want to understand – how things connect. You have a voice, but it doesn't know what to say. So you stay quiet – because you're shy. You are, and always have been, cripplingly shy. A gentle and timid person, you're not going to take the world by storm. But you move forward, one task at a time, making things happen. You're a dreamer, but also a doer. You like to build things. But not too quickly. You do things at your pace, which allows you to savour the experience. You're the parent of your creations, but always a child lost in wonderment of the world. These gifts are free. But you still want that goddam toy.

You get a job delivering Sunday newspapers.

It pays four pounds a week and takes four hours to complete. It's exhausting but enjoyable work. Those papers sure are heavy. *Words can weigh so much.* But you take pride in being the messenger. Lugging the bundles from door to door, supplying the weekly news and enduring the snarls of neighbourhood dogs, you're known as someone who delivers. You do whatever it takes. Small sacrifices for big rewards. Extra effort makes you stronger. Fitter. Wiser. You take to pulling the newspapers along on a skateboard in summer and a sledge in winter. It's faster, more efficient. You're earning more per hour, and you get to zoom down hills at the end of the day.

But it's not enough. You keep glancing at the papers. They're not yours to read – only your cargo to deliver. And deliver them you must. Quickly. Your job is to get the information across before your customers have woken, so they can enjoy a slow and leisurely read. Theirs is the pleasure, yours is the agony of delivery. You cannot let them feel your pain.

You like being the messenger. You dream of eventually delivering the mail as well. Letters are more personal than printed words; they're handwritten bonds that connect people. Plus, you'd be allowed to wear shorts to work. You like wearing shorts. They're all you've known. Next year will mark your progression to long trousers. 'Big School' beckons and with it a new dress code – and mode of conduct. First, though, you have a whole summer of cloud spotting and pond dipping to enjoy. You're a dreamer, always drifting on the breeze or swimming with the fishes. Rarely do you tread on firm soil. Yours is a world of imagination and possibility. Always creative, always free, you skip as often as you walk.

You land with a thud at Big School. You'd not done anything differently to normal. Maybe it was the dancing and singing you were doing in the playground? One minute you were flapping your arms while flying with the birds, the next you're looking down a long barrel of blurring vision as the school bully smacks your head against the pavement. The beatings continue like this. Day after day. Every break and lunchtime. Until you learn to run. And run fast. Away from your troubles. You don't stop running. Until they catch you. They are the bully and a gang of four. You plead for mercy. You make some jokes. You cower. You hold your hands to your face. You feel the pain. A blow to your stomach doubles you over. Vomit pours from your mouth. You hear their laughter. Punches become kicks as you fall to the floor. They *enjoy* hurting you. You're the ragdoll that makes them feel strong. But you're stronger. You know how to escape – into the dark recesses of your mind. The world goes black and you find safety in the silence. Later, in hospital, you're told that there are no broken bones. The bruising will fade, but the scars will last a lifetime.

You learn to find places to hide. Libraries are best. They're quiet. Peaceful. Tranquil. You love books, and the bullies don't read. You escape there to be free and never alone. The rows of shelves make order out of your chaos. Each book is a doorway to another world. It opens with a smile, knowing it is held in welcoming hands. People will say that you've retreated into your own world. But it's not true. As a ponderous type, you're someone who grows strong in the quiet of your mind. Reading is a silent and static act. Do these people not know the joy of books, the wild adventures to be had within them, and the liberating silence of a library?

Stay safe. Stay free. See beyond. You've found a place to heal, grow, and enjoy the limitless pleasure of possibility. You start yearning for, rather than fearing, the time between classes.

You're twelve years old and in love with stories. How many books have you read? Several hundred. Not that you're counting them. You're *reading* them. You adore language. You marvel at the writing styles of different authors. You know what reads well and what doesn't. Most importantly, you *feel* the words. They flow through your heart and mingle with your soul. They fuel your passions and feed your ideas. Their messages carry you to places where the words and letters disappear, leaving images vividly imprinted upon your mind. It's here that you construct and conduct the impossible. 'Worlds within words' becomes your mantra as you search for the next title to read.

Every day and at every opportunity, you read. You've just finished *The Chronicles of Narnia*, *The Lord of the Rings* and *Tarka the Otter*. The power of imagination, the mystery of the past, the magic of nature; they're as fantastic as the worlds of make-believe that have enabled you to survive your tormented reality. But the threat of beatings and humiliation no longer fuels your time in the library. You're there for the discovery. You read this, and that, and everything you can. All styles. All genres. Books are portals to new dimensions, accessed through the quiet of your mind.

The library, as you begin to hear, is not silent. There's a whispering call in each book that sounds as you turn the page. You begin reading each chapter several times before you move on. Fuelled by a curiosity you can't explain, you start looking for the 'how' as much as the 'what' on the page. The writer's craft is there, in black and white, for you to see. You study it. Every. Last. Word. Every comma and mark. You *study*. They are the code of freedom and a route map to your future.

It's time for you to pick up the pen that will become your wand. You are about to become a writer.

With eyes closed, you begin thinking and feeling – reaching out for the message and words to use. They're there, in the nothingness of your mind, waiting to form. You reach further and feel the hand of the muse that will guide you. From darkness comes light. Nothing becomes something. Words form, and you speak through your pen. It and you are connected. You feel completely, heart-poundingly, *alive*. Yet, as before, you're only the messenger. You'll only ever be the messenger – between muse and audience. Always humble, you speak to and for others. Theirs is the leisure; yours is the eventual pleasure. For now, though, writing is tough.

Communication should be easy. At least that's what you keep telling yourself as you fumble for the right words and sentence structures to adopt. Your first attempts are little more than infantile babble. But instead of the 'Da-Das' and 'Ma-Mas' of a baby, you feel compelled to use long words and long sentences. They sound unnatural and don't pause for breath. Some words are misspelled or misused. They're exhausting to write and awkward to read. You're trying *too hard*. The voice on the page is not yours. You stop and reflect, seeking to learn from your mistakes. It's this act – of stopping, reflecting, learning, and doing things better – that becomes the daily habit that will drive your future successes. But you don't know this yet. For now, you're stumped by whether and how to use an em dash or semicolon. Damn, grammar is tough.

Fortunately for you, you're in a library with a whole section on English language. You've read these books (too many for you to comprehend) and have learned that the more you read, the more you realise how little you know. It's going to take time to study and practise this craft. But it won't stop you finding your voice and speaking out. An audience would rather hear you speak poorly than wait uncomfortably for your first stuttering words. *The longer the wait, the more awkward the communication.* So you write a daily diary, just to get into the habit of sharing your thoughts and observations in writing. Pen...to...paper. That's the trick. Keep it up. Keep getting better. You know you can do it.

You're thirteen before you can write as fluently as you can speak. Not a bad apprenticeship, though of course you're still only taking baby steps. But you're pleased. It took the first two years of your life for you to learn how to say your first words, and eleven more to speak fluently with a broad vocabulary. But you're not cocky. You know that writing requires continuous practice if it's to flow naturally for you and your reader. But it's only communication. If you know how to speak, and are clear about what you want to say to whom, then you can learn how to write.

To your surprise, you learn that – with time on your side and plenty of thought – writing is easier than speaking. Unlike speaking, writing can be done as slowly as you like. You're in greater control, having more time to think about, construct, rest, proofread and edit your message before it's shared. Rarely do you get this luxury with speaking. You realise that all your concerns about word choice, grammar, punctuation, clarity, pace, story, characterisation and dialogue can be resolved by taking your time. Your process? 'Clarity of message. Simplicity of language.' Say what you mean to say. The rest can follow. And, unlike speaking, you can get someone to check your writing before you share it. English teachers and editors are good for things like that.

Your favourite tutor at school is a grey-haired and steely-eyed lady who teaches English Language and Literature. She's Head of English, so commands authority with terrifying strictness. Her pupils make sure they've prioritised her homework over that set by other teachers. This troubles some of your classmates, but not you. You love her subjects and, connecting through the beauty of the printed word, love your English teacher too. She's the mentor who's shaping your schooling like nobody else, getting you to read things that are enhancing your view of the world. Also, inspired move that it is, she gets you to do the quick crossword in the newspaper every day until you're well-practiced in using a thesaurus. You're growing as a writer and custodian of words, devoted to your teacher and the tasks she sets you. No wonder you get straight 'A' grades in her subjects. You couldn't possibly let her down.

School is good for you. The bullies have finally left you alone and you're exploring the gifts of knowledge and independent thinking that quality education provides. You're free to dream and flourish, using language to connect things. So, knowing that you learn best by doing, you decide to write a book. Not a massive tome, just enough to prove to your teacher – and yourself – that you can do it. Where, then, to start?

Learning is easiest when you're shown how to do it. So you start by copying the work of others. Artists and musicians do this, so why not writers? Your favourite authors are Tolkien, Lewis, Dahl and Pratchett. So you borrow characters from their books, placing them into a dark world of tunnels and dungeons hidden beneath a foreboding castle. You're copying, but it's your book. The rules are yours to make, applying whatever twists you like. Such is the whim of fancy that spills from an inventive mind. So, in your book, Gandalf carries a vial of marvellous medicine, Prince Caspian has a magic ring, and Mort wonders why he's developed such large hairy feet. There's humour throughout, soberly balanced by the prospect of loss, but the book is about moving forward – going deeper to find your treasure and eventual escape. It's much the same as your journey at school, but you're unable to grasp the responsibility of narrative. So you elect not to tell a story. Instead you end each chapter with options for the reader to progress.

If they choose 'Route 1' then they turn to a specific chapter, 'Route 2' will take them elsewhere. Ultimately they'll come to either a painful end or a golden treasure. It's their choice, their fate, so you can't be blamed for the blood-filled pits, lava-pooping dragons and sex-craved she-ogres that await them.

You share the book with your English teacher. She reads it and, without you knowing, passes it to her colleague who runs the school's *Dungeons & Dragons* club. He loves it so much that he photocopies the book for each member of the club. Twenty facsimiles are produced, including a card-backed version for you. You receive it the following day, when you're invited to sit with the club at their special table in the school canteen. You're hailed as the school's first author and given a complimentary burger and chips for your effort. This, in its small way, is your first book launch and taste of publishing – even if it came with ketchup and the association of hanging out with the school's biggest nerds. As you bite into your burger, you see your English teacher smiling at you from across the room. She and you know that this is the beginning of your future. Because, great teacher that she is, she's got something bigger planned for you.

You finish your lunch and, while the canteen empties of pupils, your English teacher approaches. She's had an idea: "Let's publish a school newspaper," she says. "I'll sponsor it and a handpicked team will write it. You and my other top student will edit it. The project will be good for you, in many ways." She smiles, then leaves you to ponder her proposal.

Words, as you are beginning to learn, have an ability to grow legs and run — so that you don't have to — even if you're inclined to stay put. Once they're out there, they speak for themselves. Such is the power, influence, responsibility and burden associated with a writer's platform. Private writing is one thing, but putting your name to something that is accessible to others? That's something else. Especially when the other top English student is a confident, charming, intelligent and deeply attractive person with brown eyes and a smile that melts your heart. Together you'd be the dream team, even if you'd find it impossible to stop dreaming of each other.

Teenage love, as you discover, is not as blind as some would think. You accept your English teacher's proposal, form your team, and begin work on the school's first newspaper. It teaches you about journalism, photography, desktop publishing, commercial printing, and how to prevent others from knowing that you've started dating your co-Editor. It's very much a labour of love, with headlines you'll never forget.

The newspaper, and your romance, is short-lived. You leave school for college and face the challenges of young adulthood. You're on unfamiliar ground, with new people and more challenging assignments, but you're still studying English. Your college library is 'okay' but the town library is excellent. Being a loner doesn't help you to make many friends. You're the geek with the book who's always in the library. You feel your heart grow heavy as your arms cling tightly to each other. You're a huddle of one, alone in the cold, with 'only' words for company. You've been here before, but not feeling like this. Teenage hormones? Emotions? Neediness? Loss of your first love? No. Writing is your first love. You're just feeling the first pangs of sadness that, as a sensitive person, come to punctuate your life.

Grounded in depression, you read and write to hold on to the light. The poet, as you learn, must feel the pain. Ignoring it is to only partially live. You begin reading and writing poetry, learning that from sorrow comes joy – 'lilacs bred from the dead land'. Poems help you to explore your sense of self and place in the world. New tools become available for your writing. Techniques such as content and form, intent and interpretation, rhythm, rhyme, metre, are used to aid understanding and convey meaning. You start thinking in verse, and writing with fewer words. You write a book of poems, but it's too dark to read. You tape it up and hide it on the top shelf of your bookcase, wishing it to be lost forever. But it's you who feels lost, even though you're finding yourself in new ways.

Writing *is* poetry. Worlds within words, messages between lines, one's soul on the page and one's visions in the mind of one's reader. You feel this and connect with the poets. You know that reading and writing moves you. Wordsworth, Byron, Shelley, Keats, Eliot and Plath become your friends. You find your soulmates and hope that one day, when you've published a book, your readers will find the same in you. You just need one person, *someone*, to hear you. Whatever, wherever and whenever you write, you're doing it for them. You're always writing, imagining, that someone is hearing your words and understands. Friendship, you hope, is bound by and between the covers of books. You're there, together, because you both understand. Words are your way of always being there for each other.

University encourages you follow your head more than your heart. You pursue your artistic interests but don't study English. It's a mistake that you'll always regret. But you befriend someone with blonde hair and blue eyes who is studying English. This person steals your heart and fires your passion for writing. You dearly love them, but could never tell them. Instead, you cloak your emotions and true self in bravado. Too afraid that honesty will expose you to hurt, you keep your feelings in check. Thankfully you still have the written word to keep your heart beating. You write to your friend during the holidays. They always reply. You love these letters more than all others. Your heart flutters when they arrive and you're breathless as you read them. They say everything, and mean everything, except the one thing you hope for and fear: that there's a connection beyond mere words. So you choose your words carefully in your replies. Never has your writing been so meticulously edited, or so many drafts written, before it is shared. You speak, but don't speak truth. It hurts, and you learn to never again write like this. (How foolish the editing process can be when it removes the intended message. Freedom of expression should always be free. If you love someone or something, then say it. There's every chance that you won't have to say why.)

University encourages you to write differently, and for new audiences. You see an opportunity to rewrite your college brochures and course prospectuses. You'd observed that they were poorly written. They didn't speak to the reader, or explain why the university was different to or better than others. Most of all, they didn't appear to understand the benefits sought by prospective students. You make it your mission to know and understand your audience before speaking to them.

Given that studying is an act of investing in one's future, you discover that prospective students would rather know about what's happening today, and where the university and its students are heading, than what it offered a hundred years ago. It takes you two weeks to rewrite the copy, and only a year for the university to double its number of applicants.

The pen, you discover, is mightier than the sword – so long as it's never far from a chequebook. Organisations will pay good money in return for more money. Alas, you don't get paid for your efforts. But it makes you wonder whether there could be a career in writing this sort of thing.

Soon you have a diploma on the wall and letters after your name. They qualify you to do menial work typical of many graduate jobs. You get a job as a designer. It's an income that brings you into regular contact with people but pays very little. You discover that you're a better listener and empathiser than your colleagues. It's easy for you connect requirements with solutions. But you're doing this verbally and visually rather than through the printed word. It's not enough. Writing's what you're good at, what you enjoy. It defines you, completes you. Anything less leads to a lack of fulfilment that saps you of energy. If you're not writing, you're not living.

Writing is the most important thing in your life. It has to come first. But you still have to do what other people call 'living'. You're writing diaries and letters that require you to build a bank of experiences. So you treat 'living' as research for your writing. It helps you to maintain a healthy balance but, by gum, it sure takes up valuable writing time. The best way to remain productive, you discover, is to write before the distractions of the day take hold. You rise at 4.30am and write by candlelight until 7.30am (when you eat your breakfast and then leave for work). That's three hours of quality uninterrupted writing time before most folk are awake. You're living in the twilight, mining a seam of creativity in the cocoon of isolation. It's pure, perfect, bliss. Three hours: enough to write a chapter in your diary or six letters to your friends. How many words? You average two thousand per session. This is your new routine, your unbreakable habit, your morning output and your lifelong commitment to being a writer. Writing is a *serious* business. You learn never to approach your writing desk with anything other than complete commitment and absolute focus.

But you're still only a part-time writer, at least in your mind. Your day job has changed: you've been back to college and retrained in the craft of helping organisations to engage with customers. It's called marketing. You know this. You've read the textbooks and sat the exams. You wear the badge of the person who understands what people want, what benefit they seek, and how to articulate value better than the competition. These are essential skills for a would-be author and publisher, but you can't forge the link, even though you're working as a copywriter. Writing to you is about freedom of expression – being as creative as possible – to write the unexpected. Copywriting seems formulaic and boring. You follow brand guidelines and kowtow to Legal. You play safe and homogenise your messages to appeal to a broad audience. It dilutes the impact of your words. They limp rather than run, but gather enough value to help you pay the rent. But you're barely making ends meet.

You're living in near-squalor in a converted attic. There's more damp than space, no heating or hot water, and it's infested with mice that have covered everything in urine. You're spending more time vomiting into the toilet than eating, so you're losing an alarming amount of weight. But you keep going.

Supercharged by caffeine tablets and energy drinks, you're working twenty hours per day and surviving on two hours sleep a night. You're maintaining your morning writing ritual, but you're getting sluggish and your hands are starting to shake. You begin to resent your work and hate the irony of your life: that writing is stopping you from writing.

Your output tells a different story. Your copywriting has attracted unprecedented interest in your employer's services. They experience growth like never before. You win awards, journalists interview you, experts fly in from across the globe to learn from you, and universities ask you to guest lecture. People want to understand the secrets of your success. You have Golden Rules and insist on speaking clearly, but the magic is difficult to describe. You're hailed as the best at what you do. Your face appears in recruitment campaigns saying 'you too could be as successful as this'. But it's meaningless. Crowds are flocking to you, but you've never felt more alone. In amongst the celebrations, your muse has gone silent and your ego has taken over. Empty within, you crumble under the weight of your success. You cease writing a diary and stop writing to your friends. You've become so good at the 'how' that you've forgotten your 'why'. You're still the gentle kid cowering before the bullies. Only this time the punches are your own, aimed right back in your face. You sink once more into darkness. It's six months before you function again.

There's someone from college who still remembers you for who you were, before your 'reputation' took hold. You meet up. You talk about writing. You rediscover your passion. You fall in love. You get married. You commit to never again compromising your beliefs or doing anything that offends your soul. You will rebuild your life, living on your terms. Everything you do will support your 'why' – that you are an author. You gaze at your little book of wizardry from school that sits on your bookshelf. It was the first but won't be the last. New and weightier tomes will eventually join it. You have a message to share and a voice with which to speak. It's time for you to be heard. Your time, is now.

You make the bravest leap of your life: penning and publically sharing writing that bears your name. No more hiding behind an employer or ghost-writing someone's conference speech. You're doing this on your own

– standing up, speaking out – waiting to be shot at, but moving forward quicker than the bullets can catch you. From now on you're a writer. Nothing less. Professional in mindset and behaviour, you challenge yourself to see what you can achieve.

You begin writing a series of journals, each one covering a subject close to your heart and accounting for a year of your life. To cement your commitment to being an author, you ensure that one of them tracks the year in which you decide to follow this path. Your 'writer's year' will be a little book that starts with the basics of writing – the art of picking up a pen and using it to commit your thoughts to paper – then will delve into the writer's craft, tools, and lifestyle. You know that every time you pick up a pen and write, you become the person you're meant to be. Pen choice, therefore, is important. But not as much as the message and lifestyle it enables. You know that to be a successful writer you have to be passionate about your subject, obsessively compelled to write (and write well), and fearless in your quest to share your words – regardless of what others might do to stop you. Without these three things, you might as well be writing with ice on a hot day. Success equals impact. It's up to you how broad you wish this impact to be.

You resume your morning routine, writing two thousand words before breakfast, and write a further fifteen-hundred at night when your other half has gone to bed. Within two years you've written more than a million words that will form the basis of fourteen books, two self-help guides and three screenplays. It's valuable and marketable collateral. Surely a publisher would be interested? You research the market, identifying agents and publishers within your genre. You buy books on the publishing process and how to write the 'perfect' pitch. You learn that the publishing market is fiercely competitive, because it's easy to enter. Traditional print publishers are suffering due to the popularity of eBooks and competition from self-published authors. They're still the best at marketing, distributing and protecting their legal assets, but they're difficult to contact. They only deal with agents, and these agents seek to make a living by taking a percentage of the author's royalties. If the author isn't going to sell enough books to generate a commercially viable cut for the agent, then their pitches are rejected – however well written they are.

You know that you're an unknown and undiscovered author who writes non-fiction for a niche market. Your books are unlikely to compete for shelf space with JK Rowling or John Grisham. But you seek to be a 'proper' author. Something in your psyche tells you that to be working with anything other than a major publishing house is a sign of failure. So you draft your pitch letters and send them to six agents at a time. The rejection slips mount up, all explaining that you have promise but lack marketability. It seems that to succeed in the non-fiction space you have to be a celebrity or high profile expert in your field. Prospective book buyers have to know and trust your reputation and be actively searching for you. The way to do this? You have to build an extensive and credible author platform. You don't have this yet, so you scale back your aspirations.

You approach several niche publishers to see if they'll

publish your books. All of them agree to help you, but offer terrible commercial arrangements. Some want you to cover all their costs, some will split the costs, and others will cover their costs but guarantee no earnings for you. The best will provide you with a one-off payment that would barely cover the cost of your time writing the first chapter. It seems that publishers, large and small, are risk-averse and play safe with 'bankable' authors that readily fall into established and growing pigeonholes. These holes tend to be dark, full of feathers and crusted in poo. Are they where you want to be?

Money aside, it surprises you to learn that the author – not the publisher (generally speaking) – is responsible for promoting their books. The publisher's sales team will help to push your titles into bookshops, but it would be your responsibility to pull people into the shops to buy your books. You don't have a network of interested readers ready to part with their cash, so – facing reality – you realise that you're a nobody whose books will disappear into the noise and indifference of an overcrowded market. You've made a mistake, spending two years writing about a broad range of things that you love rather than focusing on a topical and commercially profitable subject. Do you even know the sales figures for books in your genre, which ones top the bestseller lists (and why) and which authors' works will compete with yours? And are these people making a good living from writing, or do they supplement their income with other earnings? You're a marketer, so you should have known better.

Promoting yourself to unknown or 'cold' markets

would be foolhardy. But you have to start somewhere. Researching them is important, but not as an excuse for not sharing your work. You need to speak out and share your words, never feeling like you're talking to an empty room. You must find and go to your readers, to be where they are. You're a writer who seeks to connect with people, so you ought not be shy. So you make it your business to know what magazines and blogs they're reading, what social media they use, which events they attend, and which authors they follow, so that you can get your writing in front of them on a regular basis. Awareness and 'top of mind' are everything. Well, so long as these people like you.

You decide to grow your reputation gradually and organically using word of mouth recommendations. You're still growing in confidence, inching forward, doing one thing at a time, learning to walk before you can run. All you need to do is find one reader with influence who's passionate enough about your writing to mention you to someone else, and so on, until the snowball of interest grows. Maybe then you'll be attractive to the larger publishing houses, but it will take time. Time you don't have. You're still living in a capitalist world, still yearning toys and a better life. So you make a decision: you will self-publish your books. It's a protracted way to do things, but puts you in control. It's also expensive, requiring investment you don't have. You'll need to get a better-paid day job to fund your new publishing empire.

You consider getting a job as a postman, to honour your childhood dream, but it would use up valuable early-morning writing time. You're most creative during the morning, before you've woken to the thoughts and stresses of day, so you protect this time. Instead you search the job adverts in the national newspapers. There's one that catches your eye. It's from a telecommunications company that's looking for someone capable of writing 'compelling stories'. You apply and, at interview, learn that the job requires you to do a special type of copywriting that's used in sales proposals and presentations. You'd be part-writer, part-editor, crafting documents that communicate value propositions from one company to another. It's much like you did before, but on a business-to-business level. No more homogenised messaging; instead an opportunity to know the exact customer and understand what value they seek. Crafting compelling stories would be easy. You accept the job and get working. Your first paycheque is a godsend. You've been living on overdrafts for two years and desperately need to clear your debts before you can fund your publishing activities. Still, you manage to put enough aside from your first pay packet to purchase a special fountain pen. It's a token of your commitment to becoming a writer. You promise that one day it will feature on the cover of your writing book.

Your new job teaches you about the brutal reality of indulgence verses necessity. There's often a difference between what you want to write versus what people will pay to read. Your creative writing to date has been anecdotal and observant of whatever was happening in your life – a craft forged of diary and letter writing. Now you're being paid by the word to write proposals that 'compel' the reader to part with their cash. This means writing 4,000 words of finished copy per day. Every day. Without fail. On top of your creative writing done each morning and evening. And if your copywriting doesn't 'compellingly' secure the business, then you're out of a job. Output and win rate are everything. It's high pressure and murder on your fingers, which ache and throb at the end of each day, but you're earning enough to start building your business. You buy a laptop and desktop computer, plus all the software needed to write and publish your books. You go on courses in desktop publishing, website design, direct marketing, and journalism. You put money aside to fund print runs and promotional campaigns. In fact, you do everything except the thing that's most needed: networking. You convince yourself that, if you can avoid distractions, you'll get all your books completed and 'out there' before you're required to spend all your time meeting and influencing people. Can they help you now? Sure they can. But you're stubborn and want to do things all by yourself. Such are the self-sabotaging limitations of an intensely shy, creative perfectionist.

You apply the same rules and professionalism to your creative writing as to your day-job. If your current project is no better than the one that came before it, or if your output drops, then you've stagnated as an artist. Always challenging yourself to grow, innovate and perfect what you're doing, you push yourself to be the best you can be. This requires you to be hypercritical of your work. There's no room for indulgence, no pampering to your whims. 'If the writing's not good enough, it gets the cho-.'

Eventually you've amassed the skills and resources to publish a book. You start by launching a website that features some of your work and encourages visitors to sign up to your mailing list. You guest blog on websites whose visitors match your target audience. You write for magazines. You build your social media profile. You send press releases to influencers, publishers and broadcasters. You obsess about building awareness and a loyal following. Self-publishing or not, you need this author platform.

You work to your means and available time, noting that book publishing and promotion takes two-three times longer than it did to write the books. And the books themselves? You can only afford to produce them in magazine format. But they're high quality and worthy of collection. So you release them as limited edition 'preview' print runs that will pave the way for hardbacks and paperbacks. You sell eight thousand copies. It's great validation of your appeal as an author, but you've barely covered your costs. People will only pay so much for a magazine. eBooks are next, outselling the magazines 7:1 and helping to maintain a trickle of money, but you dread the day when you have to fund hardbacks and launch to the mass market. You don't have the money or space to print and store tens of thousands of books. And even if you did, distributing them would be a full-time job. You're a writer. You did your delivery work when you were ten years old.

Print-on-demand is your saviour. Improvements in print quality and distribution mean that you can employ a third party to print and ship your books as demand arises. You need only do the writing, editing, book design and promotion. The third party does the rest. There's no cash flow or stock holding concerns. You just add an ecommerce plug-in to your website and let them fulfil the order. Suddenly you're a publisher who can scale to meet global demand. Overseas sales grow to the point where only ten per cent of your readers are in your home country. You're an internationally successful author – the one most people have never heard about. But it's not about volume, always depth of connection. You're only ever speaking to one reader at a time.

Keeping your day job separate from your creative writing is becoming increasingly difficult. You're spending all morning writing, all day writing, and all evening promoting your books. You're back working a twenty-hour day, doing two jobs. But it doesn't feel like work. It energises you. Sleep becomes a frustrating burden – because it takes you away from your writing desk. You're addicted to the activity. The quality of your output is better than ever. But it comes with a warning: your two very different types of writing are clashing with each other. Your day job requires a writing style and persona that's tough, hardworking, and ruthlessly competitive; your 'out-of-hours' writing allows you to gently flutter on the breeze of creativity, finding inspiration in the ether of the possible. They are unhappy bedfellows. You wrestle with the challenges of identity and brand, doing your best to prevent your two personas from overlapping. You elect to use your real name for work and a pen name for your books. It helps you to keep your writing styles distinct and authentic. You realise, however, that this is only part of the problem. The real issue is that you're alone. You need someone to help you.

You crave having a mentor, someone who can guide you and open doors to the publishing industry. You know several authors with agents, but none offer their help. It seems that the more successful you appear, the more they see you as competition. This jealousy, in its silent way, is the very worst kind of writer's block. Friendships sour because of it. Eventually you find a professional coach to help you. He's not a writer or publisher, but he understands personal development and the achievement of goals. He also knows the importance of meaningful connections and 'making a difference by being different'. He gets you to revisit your message and rethink your brand, helping you to define what you want to say, to whom, how, and by when. And he holds you to your commitments, not allowing you to stray or slow down. You find your mission. This, through its simplicity (which says, "You're a writer, does it matter whether you're writing for yourself or others?") enables you to bring together all of your writing activities. You tell your colleagues at work about your creative writing, and your readers about your day job. Suddenly you have a new vein to mine, writing about a complete life that acknowledges the pressures and pleasures of work and home. You revisit and rewrite your books, sewing a thread of continuity through them that highlights your brand promise: that these books will, in their own little way, help your reader to find freedom – just as you did in the school library all those years ago. You've become a lifestyle author whose insights are born from experience and a different view of the world. You've found your 'angle' and unique voice. People start to listen and take notice. You win more awards. You're asked to coach others. For the first time in your life, you don't have to chase the work. Offers start coming in to give talks and write articles. You spend three years travelling the world, telling your story and encouraging people to follow their dreams. Most importantly, you're providing them with the tools to achieve success. Like the teacher who once encouraged you to take bigger steps, so you are helping them to stand tall. You make them laugh, you make them cry, you make them think and act. You know that as a writer and public speaker, your audience will forget your words but remember your story and how you made them feel. This is the writer's gift. You're a storyteller, entertainer and educator. Uncomfortable being the narrator of someone else's life, you base your stories on your experiences and allow your readers to make choices for themselves. Such are the freedoms of expression and interpretation.

You pause to reflect. You're forty years old. Six years have passed since you wrote a book about writing and two since you began self-publishing. You've held down a full-time writing job throughout. So here you are, proud in the knowledge that you've fulfilled your destiny. You're a full-time professional writer. You've published thirty million words in your career and have just earned your first million as a writer. There will be more, but you're mindful that these numbers will alienate some people while encouraging others. You choose to include them in the extended version of your book so that your reader knows that dreams *can* be achieved through the application of hard graft, skill, and focus. Mostly it requires constant self-belief, self-encouragement (never rely on others to chivvy you along), self-determination, honest perspective, avoidance of distractions, and above all else: a pure love of reading and writing.

You'll always read more than you write, doing so feeds the well of your writing. Your books pay homage to all the great writers and teachers who've imparted the gift of language upon you. And so you pass the pen to whomever reads your books. But to fully understand your story, they need to go back to the year that made it happen. When you wrote a book about your writer's year.

Stop – Unplug – Escape – Enjoy

How will you define and measure your success?

II

A ROOM FULL OF BOOKS

Welcome to a place where the only sound is that of footsteps across floorboards and the 'shhh-tru' of pages being turned. Where lives are bound to silent wonderment and worlds open up in the palms of one's hands. Welcome, to the timeless zone of the bookshop.

I'm writing this in the corner of a bookstore in Hay-on-Wye, the mecca for book-lovers worldwide. The bookseller has given me permission to sit here and write, so long as I agree to purchase a book before I leave. It's a good deal, especially as I've spied an 1897 first edition of *The Idle Thoughts of an Idle Fellow* by Jerome K. Jerome. I'm something of an idle thinker, but not an idle fellow. Often you'll see me in an apparent state of laziness, gazing into nowhere as I reach into my thoughts for inspiration, but I'm being far from lazy. As a writer, I'm always writing or thinking of what to write. Such is the creative gift – and curse – of a mind that's always switched on and set to full volume. This is why bookshops are great for writers: they're quiet places, free from distractions, and only a page turn away from new ideas.

As someone who's equally passionate about reading as writing, I know that the flow of words into one's mind helps to swell one's creative output. It's like an exchange system between authors. They fill one's artistic reservoir, grease one's inventive cogs, and before you know it you're writing full pelt as the writing machine spins into action. So I'm always interested to see bookshelves belonging to writers. What books do they own? How many of them have they read? Which ones look like they've been read most often? What's the ratio between books read and books written? And that's just the numbers game. The real interest is in seeing what books they *read*. On what subjects, by which authors, in which genres and in which eras? Do they store them neatly in pristine bookcases, like lawyers showcasing their knowledge, or are they stacked higgledy-piggledy in an 'always to hand' fashion? Whichever it is, one can never have enough books, or reading time, or writing time. Such is the uncontainable pleasure of words and the magic of a good story.

One's library and writing space says a great deal about us. It inspires and encourages us into action. How great it must be to have a book of our own to sit alongside the tomes of our favourite authors? This is the not-so-secret desire of the would-be author, especially when the book is stored in the perfect writing place. The best writing place I've ever seen was discovered ten years ago.

Back in 1998, my friend Phinehas was looking to move from his townhouse in Birmingham to a 'writer's retreat' in the Welsh countryside. He'd grown tired of city life and wanted to live "out of other people's hair". He craved the simple life, but not a meagre one. A man of comfortable means, he wanted a property with moderate luxury and a twist of elegance – such as a Victorian sporting lodge on a rural estate. Somewhere he could forget the stresses of life and surrender himself to the movements of his pen.

Phinehas asked me if I could help him view a 'rather special' house. He'd already viewed it but needed someone to help him make up his mind. I agreed, and that weekend we travelled to Wales together. Our journey took us from the West Midlands conurbation though the fruit-growing counties of Worcestershire and Herefordshire, and finally into Powys. We reached the crossroads at Rhayader (the oldest town in mid-Wales) and turned left, heading south of the town along a road that ran parallel to the River Wye. We pulled over and Phinehas said, "Okay. We're here". I looked through the car window to see a slate-walled single storey building that looked no more appealing than a lock-up garage.

"Is this it?" I asked. "It looks like a cross between a toll-house and an oversized bus stop."

"Just you wait," said Phin'.

Phinehas had been coy about the property during the drive, but now began telling me about its history. "The building," he said, "was built in 1896 from slate destined for the dam of the Caban-coch reservoir in the Elan Valley above Rhayader. Its original purpose was to accommodate officials visiting to view the construction of the dams, but soon became used as a sporting lodge for Midland businessmen. It's called Nantgwyllt, after the mansion house where the poet Shelley lived in 1811. The mansion was located alongside the River Claerwen in the valley above the town, but was lost beneath the waters of Caban-coch when the valley was flooded."

"I'm beginning to see why the property appeals to you," I replied.

"Yeah," said Phinehas, "but it's also located on a sharp bend in the river. There's a salmon pool at the end of the garden."

"The penny's just dropped," I said. "You like the idea of fishing from your bedroom window."

"So-so," said Phinehas, calmly. "But it has a more impressive feature. *Just you wait and see.*"

We exited Phin's car and walked up to the front door of the property. Phin' knocked. We waited. And waited. And waited. After an age, the door opened and a short hunch-backed old lady greeted us. She smiled and, in a soft but frail voice, apologised for the delay: "It's the stairs y' see; they're too steep. This house has too many stairs. Still, I'm here now. Welcome gentleman. Please come in."

Stairs? I thought this was a bungalow?

We entered the house and I quickly found myself clinging to a banister as I descended a dimly lit and ridiculously steep staircase that started within two feet of the front door. The stairway led to a perpendicular corridor that ran the length of the house. On one side were doors leading into the downstairs rooms; on the other was shoulder-high oak panelling with whitewashed rock above.

"House's built right into the cliff" said the lady. "Solid it is, solid as them dams up in the valley. But oh, them wretched stairs. I'll be glad to leave."

She proceeded to tell us that she'd lived there since before the war, but her husband had recently passed away. "Too many memories," she said, "and too many stairs." Her goal now was to sell the house and move to Llandrindod Wells to live with her daughter. "I'm afraid you'll have to show yourselves around. I've done my stair climbing for the day. So have a look round. I'll be in the kitchen if you need me."

Phin' and I then perused the house which, in estate agent terms, was clean but 'in need of modernisation'. We liked its original features: oak panelling, high ceilings, ornate cornicing, carved stone fireplaces, floor-to-ceiling windows and stain-glass doors set in gothic archways. In fact it seemed like this Victorian house had barely aged since it was built. But, as you'd expect for two countryside writers, Phin' and I were soon outside gazing at the garden and salmon pool. It was one of those places where one could stand and, while watching the swirling eddies of the river, dream away an entire day.

"Phin'," I said, "You mentioned that I should wait and see. Well, I'm waiting, but I'm not sure if I've seen what I'm looking for?"

"Turn around," he said, "and tell me what you see."

I turned away from the river and back to the house. There it stood in all its Victorian splendour: two storeys high, built into the cliff behind, with eight windows top and bottom and a turret-style protrusion at the northern end.

"Do you remember going into the turret?" asked Phinehas.

"No," I replied. "I remember the bedrooms and bathroom upstairs, but not a turret."

"Then it's time I showed you."

We walked back up to the house and into the kitchen where the old lady was waiting.

"I suppose you want to see the writing room again?" she said to Phinehas. "Well you know where to find the door, so you'd best make your own way there. I'm not going to attempt it, not with all those stairs."

Phinehas led me back into the corridor at the rear of the house. "What do you see?" he said.

"Four doors, some oak panelling and not enough light bulbs," I replied.

"What about this?" he asked. He then leant gently against one of the oak panels. I heard a 'clunk' and the panel popped ajar. Phin' pulled open the panel, which revealed a dark passageway carved into the rock behind. It looked cold and uninviting – like a broom cupboard for a troglodyte housemaid. Phinehas then reached inside the entrance and I heard a click as a light bulb illuminated an eight-foot length of tunnel that curved sharply to the left.

"Okay," said Phin', "best to duck. It's a low ceiling, so you go first."

I stooped and, bending my knees, shuffled into the tunnel. The slate walls felt cold and the light bulb next to my head seemed worryingly dim, as if the wiring could fail at any moment. The passageway turned to the left and I saw a steep spiral staircase carved into the rock. I climbed thirty or so steps before reaching a door at the top. I pushed it open and was immediately dazzled by sunlight. As my eyes adjusted I began to make out an octagonal room, ten feet across and covered in dust. I walked in and surveyed the scene. The door behind me formed the rear face of the octagon; on either side of the door were floor-to-ceiling bookcases – two on one side and one on the other – which contained hundreds of gilded leather-bound books; a curved leather-topped writing desk was flush to the three sides of the octagon opposite, above which were rectangular-paned leaded windows. A captain's chair stood before the desk and on the right-hand wall was a fireplace and wood-burning stove. A burgundy red octagonal rug filled the centre of the room, around which was oak flooring.

"One could sit at that desk," said Phinehas, who was now standing alongside me, "and survey the full panorama of the river and mountains beyond. We're looking west, down the valley, to where the sun will set and the moon will float above a misty river."

"Phin', forget the view," I said. "This room is *amazing!*"

"Look more closely," said Phinehas, "and think about what you're seeing. There's no way any of this furniture could have been carried up here through the tunnel. It's original, built in-situ. The desk fits flush to the wall; the bookshelves are bespoke. Even the rug is made-to-measure. And look at this chair: its back is carved with salmon, deer, acorns and oak leaves. Carved, no doubt, in this very room by a master craftsman."

"Yes," I said, "but look closer than that. Other than the dust everywhere, it seems like the room was vacated only this morning. There's newspaper in the stove, books left open on the desk; there's even a fountain pen with its cap removed. It looks like someone popped downstairs and never came back. But it's so dusty, like no one's been up here in decades."

"Take a look at the newspaper in the stove. Is there a date on it?" said Phin'.

I opened the door of the wood-burner and removed one of the scrunched-up balls of paper. It was stiff and yellowing. I teased it open. There, in the top corner, was a date: Monday 17th October 1938.

"Sixty years!" I exclaimed, "How can something be left untouched for so long?"

"The lady downstairs and her late husband," said Phin', "decided to leave things as they found them when they moved in. They knew that the previous owner was a writer, and this was his creative room, but they didn't much care about it."

"Less me guess. Something to do with the stairs?"

"Probably," replied Phinehas. "I asked the old lady last week and she said that neither she nor her husband made any attempt to find out what the writer wrote in this room."

"If we had more time," I said, "we could look through the drawers in the desk, or flick through the books on the shelves, attempting to find out. But it would be a crime to disturb something that's been left untouched for so long."

"That's why I brought you here," said Phin'. "To show you this room, and for you to disturb the paper in the stove. I tried, but couldn't do it. It just seemed so…perfect."

"Because of that," I replied. "You'd better buy the place."

"I won't be buying it," said Phin'.

"But you've got to!" I replied. "This place is *fabulous*. It's meant to be!"

"Sorry Fen', it's too close to the road."

"But you could write anything in here. Anything at all."

"I could, but it would be impossible for me to stop gazing at the view from the windows. I'd end up as dusty as this furniture."

Phin' was right. The view from the room was too great a distraction. A writer must eventually cease the flow of input before he or she 'zones out' and commits words to paper. At least, that was my opinion at the time.

Ten years have passed. Phinehas eventually bought a writer's retreat in the south of France. But that house in Wales, with its secret writing room, features regularly in my dreams. To this day, every time I prepare myself to write, I close my eyes and imagine myself in that room. First I run my fingers along the books, then across the stone fireplace and finally onto the leather-topped table; I then sit down at the captain's chair and look out through the leaded windows, across the lawns and river, and picture the sun setting behind the mountains. I sit there until words begin to flow and my pen touches the paper. And then I can begin. All thanks to that wonderful space – that secret room – full of books and dreams.

Stop – Unplug – Escape – Enjoy

Describe your perfect writing room.
In what ways will it inspire
you to write?

January

III

TO BE AN AUTHOR

Each of us has a secret room in which we write. It exists in our mind every time we close our eyes. We sit there, encouraging the flow of words and ideas to pour forth. It's a dream, but as with all dreams, it's as real as we want to make it. My dream, the one that most encourages me, is that someday I'll see my writing in print. By this I mean a proper book that bears the name and messages of my choosing. Actually, not just a book, but a whole series linked by the themes of freedom, identity, nature, creativity, and adventure. And, ideally, they'll be books that people buy and *read*. Publishing them would mark my transition from being a writer to an author. Oh, the joys of being a *proper* author.

If, when I am older, I shall wear purple, then if I write a bestseller I shall wear fine tweeds and a silk cravat. I shall spend all day lounging in a padded leather chair, sipping expensive wine and dictating my thoughts to an army of personal assistants. My pens will be warmed in the heaving bosoms of nubile students eager for me to teach them my craft. Critics will clamour to read and love my work. My life will be a blur of book tours, celebrity interviews and cocktail parties.

Yeah, right.

The reality of being a successful author, I would imagine, is far from the stereotypical image of someone in tortoiseshell glasses who publishes a bestseller every year. It's still a job. Deadlines would have to be met and books sold. Pressure to perform would, perhaps, be greater than many day jobs. There'd be no excuse for writer's block. Publishers would demand a sense of urgency and self-discipline that could crush someone with a nine-to-five mentality. Personal sacrifice would go with the job. One would write, get paid, and then write some more. Life would be an endless barrage of words, editor's remarks and critics' flailings. Then, if word spread, one might connect with a reader or two. It would be a hard life. But we writers crave it anyway. For the recognition, the lifestyle, the legacy, and – sometimes – the money.

As I see it, there's a difference between being a writer and being an author. A writer has to write. The creative spark keeps igniting ideas that wake him or her in the night and results in notebooks being left in every room of the house. To be an author is to have that writing published, which triggers all the usual production, sales, marketing and commercial activities of a business enterprise. Being an author, therefore, is to have a toe in the creative pool and a foot in the vat of commerce.

Being able to make a living from writing, at least from book sales, is not easy. Many of my author friends exist on less than the minimum wage. But what they sacrifice in earnings they gain in lifestyle. Being able to work when and wherever they choose – be it a study, garden shed or park bench – gives them the flexibility to exist in a way that matches the mood of the day. How nice it must be to lie in bed each morning and think, "Hmmm, I wonder where I shall write today?" Sunny days might be spent outdoors, lying on a picnic blanket, chewing on a grass stalk and scribbling away; wet or cold days might be spent inside beside an open fire in the quiet corner of a pub, writing on a beer mat. Where the writing takes place doesn't matter to a publisher, but it matters a great deal to the author.

An artist friend of mine spends every summer in the French Riviera, selling his paintings to tourists. He earns enough to return to his native Wales each winter, where he lives a simple life in a cottage by the coast. He's worked and lived like this for thirty years. His life is the perfect balance of productivity, commercial success and time for himself. Often I have seen him in his front garden in Wales, sitting in the sun with his feet up, smoking a cigar and drinking a mid-morning Martini. It's all part of his daily routine that helps him to keep things real. His mantra, which he imparts to passers-by, is: "I like to start slowly, then ease up as the day progresses". It's had a lasting impression on me, proving that one can be productive and successful by pacing oneself while still making time for the niceties of life.

Life doesn't have to be a relentless, blindfolded sprint into a brick wall. If you're smart and remain focused on what's important, you can enjoy the best of everything that's on offer. All that's needed is a little routine.

I'm going to test this tomorrow, when I have a 'homeshirking' day. I've decided that atmospheric conditions will be such that there will be no mobile phone signal. Ravenous starlings will have pecked through the telephone lines, and an apprentice road worker will have dug through anything else that might enable the outside world to contact me. I am planning an author's day, defined by routine, output, and balance.

My plan for tomorrow is this: the day will begin just before dawn with a walk along the lanes near to home. I'll pause at my favourite stile in the hedgerow to watch the sunrise. I'll then sit on the stile and make notes for the writing I'll do later in the day. I'll return home and enjoy a pot of tea and a simple breakfast: bubble and squeak with two fried eggs. I'll then 'retire' to my study where I'll sketch out the storyboards for a few chapters, probe ideas and work up angles for my observations. 'Elevenses' will see me back in the kitchen making a brew, and then walking around the garden with a mug of tea in my hand. Then it will be back into my study to write the first draft of the chapter. Lunch will be a cheese ploughman's and a pint of ale at my local pub. While eating, I'll be reading and editing what I've written that morning. I'll then take a leisurely walk back to my cottage where I'll make another pot of tea before finalising the chapter. Afternoon tea will be taken in the garden, and I'll read aloud my day's output. If the weather's nice then I'll stay in the garden, making my final edits or drafting more ideas. Mrs H will return from work and then, after dinner, she and I will go for a walk along the river. We'll then come home to read our books before Mrs H heads to bed and I return to my study. I'll then write until I can stay awake no longer.

My plan is as idealised as it gets, and it will probably

change once I start writing or get disturbed. (Never, ever, interrupt an author when he or she is 'in the zone', else you'll understand the real meaning of 'writer's nib'.) But the thought of tomorrow is enough to make my shoulders relax a contented smile appear upon my face. How nice it would be to exist like that. To write at one's pace, to see and experience that which matters while still meeting production schedules and the needs of a paying audience. And it can be done, as my artist friend has proved, if we stick to the routine and remember what's important.

Perhaps I should purchase that padded leather chair and order a supply of small and extremely hard to find pens? Maybe I should get some calling cards printed with the words 'Literary Genius' embossed upon them, and then phone my bank manager to prepare her for a tidal wave of royalty cheques?

No. Not just yet. First, I will start slowly, and then ease up as the day progresses.

Stop – Unplug – Escape – Enjoy

What aspect of an author's lifestyle most appeals?

January

IV

FROM ME TO YOU

Somewhere in the pecking order of communication speeds is an envelope marked 'Urgent'. Its markings are in red letters and there's a cluster of first class stamps glued to the corner. Its sender hoped for a quick delivery, but the envelope got lost beneath a wave of telegrams, faxes, text messages, emails, instant messaging, blogs and tweets. Its sender grew old and forgot about the letter.

The letter. *The humble letter.* Once the principal means of communicating in writing, it is now condemned to the dustbin that houses camera film, vinyl records, videotape and floppy disks (and may soon contain printed newspapers and the art of conversation). The world's gone digital. For me, I have a one-digit answer to that: '!'

Please, I beg of you, call me old fashioned, a traditionalist, a luddite, a dinosaur thrust into the wind tunnel of change, holding on to whatever he can. Because it's true. The thing most tightly in my grasp is the handwritten letter. Not just because of the personal touch and the excitement of sending and receiving a letter ("eeee – mail!"), but because a letter allows us to travel through time.

Keeping the letters we receive means that we can re-read them whenever we like. And when we do, we're transported through memory to when they were written. Which is why I could never 'delete' a letter. I'd much rather store them, reading them again during sentimental times when I wish to feel close to the friends that sent them. I have many from when I was a boy, sent by friends who are no longer alive. Yet the letters are as fresh and immediate now as when they were written. That's twenty-five years ago – a quarter of a century of time travel made possible by some paper, an envelope, some ink and a stamp. I read them and into my mind flash long-forgotten memories. I'm transported back in time and my friends are as they were: youthful, energetic and eager to share their adventures. It's a two-way thing, this time travelling through letters. My departed friends can speak to me now and I can see the world as it was then. They live on. I remember.

But things *have* changed. Communication is now 'instant'. Words are disposable, ruined by a series of electronic dots, dashes and bleeps. It isn't fashionable to send letters anymore; emails don't begin with 'My Dear' or end with 'Yours faithfully'. In fact there's nothing faithful about email at all. If anything, the sender is hiding behind the typed word, afraid of sharing something about his or her character that might be revealed in their handwriting.

With letter writing becoming the dying art of an eccentric, old-fashioned few, our pool of letter-writing friends grows smaller. This concerns me, as sending and receiving letters is such a lovely thing. It's a personal gesture, so I plead with you to write and send handwritten letters. Write to me, write to your friends and family, write letters to people living in the same house as you. Send them through the mail or devise your own stamp and postage system. Imagine the recipient's eyes light up when they open your letter; hear their comments of, "Oh, you shouldn't have," or, "You silly old fool", and then feel the smile form on your face. There's warmth in this letter writing and letter sending. So please do it.

And if you think I'm bonkers, I'll validate my madness by confirming that I've also taken to writing to myself. I sent the first letter last week. I placed it in an envelope, added a first class stamp, sealed it and put it in the post box. And now I'm waiting for it to arrive. Where it's gone, and why it's taking so long to get here, I don't know. But I expect, or rather hope, that it will be nicely crumpled and franked when it arrives. My intention is to leave the letter unopened for many years, so that it surprises me when I open it. But with books also providing a form of time travel, I've decided to include it here as well. So here's a copy of the letter, shared for our benefit:

7th January 2008

Mr Dear Friend,

My name is Fennel. I'm a young(ish) man embarking upon a journey. Partly into the unknown and partly into a planned-for and imagined future. A future that, by the very nature of progress, will be different to today. Although we can't always stop things from changing, it doesn't mean we have to accept change for change's sake. Some things we'll love, others we'll avoid. What's important is knowing for sure whether we like what we see as it approaches.

I read the other day that a person's make-up (their values and beliefs) is fixed by the age of 14, after which the window for influence has passed. What remains are the ever-growing courses of bricks that build one's future self. My future self is you.

Who do I imagine you to be? The person I'll become? Thinking about it, 'become' is not the right word. I'd much rather 'remain' – at least in those areas that define me – remaining true to the person I am now, albeit enhanced by the wisdom of experience. So, who am I now? I am a man who likes quiet natural places – fields, woods, lakes, rivers, mountains and moors. I like what I find there. Both outside and within. (Make time for these places. There's no need to speak. Just stop and observe.) What else? I'm a creative person who's proud to write and draw, and I love tending to my garden. These things keep me close to the earth and help steady my heartbeat. I find comfort in traditional things, not because I'm averse to new inventions, just that I find classic style more beautiful. These things are often craftsman built and capable of connecting us with times past. Which makes me feel young, not old. I'm alive. Healthy and strong enough to speak to you through time. Because, by the time you read this letter, these words will be those of the past.

The me of now is gone, replaced by the you of now. You are my child, my future self, and I'm responsible for you. What I do or don't do today will influence my future: your past and your present. It will tilt your view of the world, because you are the plate that spins and wobbles upon the sum of our dreams. I am the rod that supports you, lifting you higher.

You are the me of tomorrow. When you read these words you will become the me of your past, talking to the you of today. So, the questions I have to ask are: "Are we the same, time differences apart? Have I changed? Do you still see through my eyes and feel as I do? Or are you the ghost of me, a young person wearing old person make-up? Do I live in your veins and in your thoughts? Are your values true to mine? Do you crave to be outdoors, to be in peaceful places where you can feel the joy of creativity and hear a steady heartbeat? Or have you forgotten how to listen to the silence where you can hear everything?"

So, are you still me, older in years but young in outlook? Do you see True Beauty before you? Do you see it behind you? Does it exist within you? Most importantly, have you become the author I wish to be? I'm choosing this path for us, as of today, so did it lead to happiness?

You are the person I chose to be. The one I invested in. Time moves on and things change, but I hope to remain in you. I am your nature. I am the inner voice that makes you 'you'. I am your child within. Never dead, always living. I ask but one thing of you: listen to me once in awhile. You may be older, but I know what I'm talking about.

Take care, my child.

Fennel

I hope you understand the meaning of these words. The letter might be most relevant to me, but I'm sure that a message to your future self would contain similar themes.

It's useful to take a snapshot of who we are, and who we hope to be, so that we can either stay true to ourselves or note how far we've come. From this moment forward, I am committed to becoming an author. The journey begins here. I marked it with a letter, and it will be a 'first class' journey. So long, of course, that someone eventually delivers the mail.

February

V

HANDWRITTEN LETTERS

Excuse me if I start this chapter more slowly than usual, but I have to wait for the post to arrive. You see, the highlight of my day has gone super-nova with the arrival of someone new delivering the mail.

Ted, our old postman, retired this week. He'd worked in the village for forty-five years but left without a goodbye. We villagers were surprised at the suddenness of his departure, as he was always known for courtesy and never for speed. He chose not to ride his postman's bicycle (it had a semi-flat tyre), but would instead push it along and spend much time leaning on gateposts while talking to people he met. Because of this, the post would rarely arrive before lunchtime, often around teatime. But this didn't matter. By the time Ted knocked on the door, he'd have so much news to tell that the post became incidental to his urge to share the daily gossip.

Mrs Baines' bunions were featured regularly in Ted's updates, as did Flash Harry's latest girlfriends and Dom the Disbeliever's attempts to build an air-raid shelter in his front garden. Last week, 'Uncle' Edna's "incredibly large spuds" had grown even bigger; Little Jimmy had bought some "unnaturally white" trainers and the nudists at Number 61 had upset

Mrs Spiggot by opening their curtains on a Sunday. All healthy gossip, shared with the straight-faced honesty of a man who regularly attended church, had never married, and thought that infidelity was a brand of videocassette.

Now we have someone new delivering the mail. A woman. Young. Athletic. Firm.

Beatrix von Baum, as I call her, is a recent graduate of the Right Wing School of Postal Efficiency. Gone are mid-afternoon deliveries and jovial comments like "Mmm. Scented!" They've been replaced by letters bound with tight elastic bands, thrust through letterboxes with the flap-straining vigour of someone with a very strong grip.

Bea's arrival has sent us male villagers into frenzy. Bob Dewar now mows his front lawn in winter, Ern Fletcher's hedge is two feet lower, and Greasy Dave has started cleaning his windows. Shame on them. Yet here am I, standing adjacent to my living room window, peering through a crack in the curtain with the expectancy of the young lad who lives opposite Number 61.

I don't know how she does it, but every day for the past three days Bea' has arrived at exactly 11.26am. It is now 11.24am. Bob is mowing his lawn, Ern is clipping his hedge, and Dave is standing at his window, buffing. Ah. Here she comes, striding down the centre of the lane. Her blonde hair bounces provocatively with her every step; her long slender legs are topped with tight postal service shorts; and her – how shall we say? – 'chest' is cocooned in a puffed-up gilet. (Mmmm. 'Bodywarmer...') She's carrying a postal bag over her shoulder and, in the cool morning air, appears as a picture of delight. But alas, she wears no smile. Bea' has the steely resolve of someone approaching a high noon showdown. In fact, she has the look of a beauty queen who's just lost her crown to the only woman to be given a refund from Weight Watchers.

Okay. Update. She has passed Bob. No letters. His mower cable has sagged and is lying lifeless on the lawn. Ern has got one letter. It's a crisp white envelope that I can see says 'Congratulations'. Never has Ern been so pleased to receive junk mail. Greasy Dave got his usual stack of brown envelopes and has disappeared from the window. Bea is now approaching my cottage. I repeat. *My* cottage. She's reaching into her bag. She's pulled out a bundle of letters. For me. There! She's approaching. Coming. Now!

Oh, I'm just not up to this. I've closed the gap in the curtain and have pinned myself to the wall as I try to steady my breathing. I've heard the latch on the garden gate flick open, the crunching of footsteps on gravel and now, nothing. No flap of letterbox. No thud of envelopes hitting the carpet. No groan of employment satisfaction. Maybe she saw me? Maybe she's peering through my living room window at this moment? Maybe she had a reckless urge and is dancing naked in my front garden? Control yourself Fennel. There must be an explanation.

Knock. Knock.

Oh no. No. No. Yeeesss….

Wait a moment while I go to the door. I don't expect it to take long.

Right. I'm back. That *was* quick, and very strange. Pleasantly strange. But strange all the same. My first contact with the post 'mistress'. Let me tell you how it went:

The door opened.

"Hi, I'm Fennel. You must be our new po-"

"Number 46. Mail."

Bea' passed me the letters, then turned and walked away. Her black ankle boots creaked rhythmically as she strode off. The gravel crunched. The latch clicked. She exited into the lane, disappearing behind a hedge of hawthorn and lilac.

Number 46. Mail. Bea's voice was without inflection. Disengaging. Robotic. Specific. An economic use of words. But was it a statement or an observation? Was she talking to me or making a note to herself? I've shut the door now, but my heart is still pounding. What if she meant "Number 46: Male!" What if she was so impressed by my flat cap and tartan slippers that she was unable to speak further? What if, at this very moment, she's talking to Mrs Dunnock next-door, asking her about the suave chap in the paisley pyjamas? Forget it Fennel. You're a married man with the sexual allure of a frog sitting on an eggcup. Best that I move on and let my neighbours do the thinking. Time for me to get dressed, make a brew, and see what letters have arrived.

Today is a special day to read letters. It's my last day at home before I return to the noise and bustle of an office. I've had it easy for the past year, working mostly from a tent by a lake, but tomorrow I must attend a meeting. *Decisions are required.* So my shirt is ironed, my shoes are polished; my hair's cut short (to enable thick ears and pains in the neck) and war rations are allocated. First, though, I am a man of leisure about to unravel the mysteries of the postwoman's bundle.

I'm now sitting in the kitchen, teacup in hand and breathing calmly. I've removed the elastic bands from the envelopes and have laid everything on the table before me. The first letter is from a company selling modern bathroom suites. Their glossy tiles and chromed fittings would ruin the charm of our garden privy, so the letter is condemned to the kindling basket. The second letter is for Mrs H; the third is for me, but has red typing on it, so I'll let Mrs H deal with that one as well. (I remember Ted commenting on such a letter, saying, "Eee. Mrs Platt at the corner shop had one of those before she went away. And we've not seen her in a very… long…time.") The final two letters are what I'd hoped to receive. No harsh, typed lettering on the envelopes. No see-through plastic windows. No 'postage paid' printing. No indication of a computer masquerading as a human. Just 'gentle' handwriting that brings the envelopes to life. Blue ink on one and green ink on the other. I know that the colours of these inks are conscious decisions by their senders. They, unlike the computers spitting out thousands of cloned missives, have feelings. They care enough to be unique, take pride in sending letters, and know the true meaning of the term 'first class'. And they've cared enough to write to me. They wish to correspond. And correspond they do. I can relate to their craft of writing letters by hand.

I will now begin a four-staged process of deduction.

Firstly, I will attempt to recognise the handwriting on the envelope. Secondly, I shall guess the nature of the letter by feeling and smelling it. Is the paper textured and of quality weight? Are there any lumps indicating the inclusion of a feather, photograph or pressed leaf? Does it have the scent of pipe smoke, woodland floor or garden shed? Thirdly, what is the franking stamp on the envelope? What county, or country, is shown? Which friend lives there? Finally, I will gently slice open the envelopes with a knife from the cutlery drawer. (This is much more civilised than clicking 'Send/Receive' on an email. Think about it: *send SLASH receive*. Email is the frenzied killer of proper communication.)

The results of the deduction are as follows: The letter written in green ink has quality paper and is franked 'Wigan'. I guessed correctly that it was from my friend Bill. It is a letter about a favourite childhood pond. The letter written in blue ink smells of pipe smoke. I guessed it was from my friend Demus, but was proved wrong. It is from Ted, our old postman. He informs me that he has retired to the coast and wishes to thank Mrs H and me for our friendship. He also wishes to make a confession. He's saying… Oh. Ha! Ted. Only you would write such things. I'll repeat them here, in his words:

"…and of course I had to leave in a hurry. I'd seen my replacement: a young lady from the city. She works the early rise and keeps her head down. Doesn't stop until all's been delivered. Alas, the thought of showing her my rounds was too much to bear. So I grabbed my bike and brought it here with me. It'd be no use to her anyway. That tyre's not been firm in years…"

HANDWRITTEN LETTERS

Ted, you old rogue. You're as red-blooded and fearful as the rest of us. Nice touch, too, with your blue thoughts written in blue ink. But Beatrix is out of our league. For some reason, she makes me yearn to possess a bigger and stiffer…pen.

Stop – Unplug – Escape – Enjoy

To whom will you write your next letter, and what will it say?

February

VI

HIS NIBS

The longest meeting in history lasted for three months, nine days and four hours. At least it seemed to last that long. Its subject was 'The Beauty of the Bottom Line', a title aimed at attracting graduate recruits who sought to understand business finance. I attended thinking I'd be surrounded by female executives wishing to impress their new employer. Sadly I ended up sitting in a room full of go-getter wannabes, trainee accountants, and confused letches. It was such a dull meeting. Just like the one I'm enduring now.

My new Head of Department ('HOD' as he likes to be called) wishes to put his stamp on the business. He called today's meeting in an attempt to stir things up and leave a legacy for when he moves on up the career ladder. The invitation to the meeting arrived via email and had the subject line: "I'd like to scheudle a meeting". Scheudle? Unfortunate typo. I wasn't sure what it meant, but it sounded like something you'd do to a poodle that's about to poop on your lawn. An hour into the meeting and HOD hasn't squatted or 'left his mark', but he's getting into position. Which might explain my urge to reach for a broom.

The topic of today's meeting is: 'The Need for

Change'. My invitation to the meeting had the flattering instruction: "As our writer your job is to make complex things sound simple and simple things seem complex". From what I've seen and heard so far, HOD's proposed changes involve doing things exactly the same way as before, but giving the process a new name. (Einstein once said, "Any intelligent fool can make things bigger and more complex. It takes a touch of genius – and a lot of courage – to move in the opposite direction." So I think my skills will be used to help the intelligent fool have his way.)

The proposed name for the process is S.P.E.N.T. It stands for 'Successful Professionals Exceed National Targets'. I think the acronym G.R.U.N.T. would be more appropriate: 'Get Ready Underdogs for New Training'. The name doesn't seem to be in debate, however, other than a comment from Mrs Dawes the Marketing Manager who suggested that the letter 'E' be added at the end, to make it seem more feminine. (SPENT-E campaigns, here we come…)

Name changes like this might sound subtle, but they affect me deeply. I'm slow to accept and adapt to new things. Change bothers me. I don't cope too well with fashions, fads and urban traffic lights. I get cold sweats when a product gets moved in the supermarket and grind to a halt when I approach an unexpected traffic diversion. I survive by championing traditionalism and enjoying slow evolution (or, as I prefer to call it, 'sustained perfection'). But this can present challenges when working in the fast lane of modern business. People label me and the things I love as being old-fashioned, archaic or obsolete. As one of my colleagues commented this morning: "You are an old pot plant standing in the corner gathering dust". I was actually flattered by this. At 34 years old, I am the old hand in the team, determined to take things easier than my younger and more ambitious workmates.

Sadly, the modern corporate workplace rarely tolerates employees who express old-fashioned tastes. Traditionalism is not fashionable. It is the dog-crawl to fashion's catwalk. As much as I would love to rebel by wearing hobnail boots, breeks and a straw hat to the office, I would be laughed out of the glass-walled booths and open plan tundra. But the traditionalist in me needs to make a statement, something that reveals my old-fashioned preferences to those with a trained eye. This is why I use a fountain pen at work.

There are twelve people in the meeting right now. I can tell a lot about them from their choice of writing instrument. HOD, for example, has a platinum-banded fountain pen that's so large it could be mistaken for a polished cucumber. He would need to do a thousand finger press-ups to be able to write with such a beast. It is a pen designed for executive signatures in prestigious boardrooms. It tells everyone that its owner is the boss and that it's proud to have avoided its fate as a whale's suppository. Mrs Dawes is scribbling away with a mechanical pencil that, every so often, she clicks to 'extend the shaft'. When she's really going for it she gives a mixture of single and double clicks that sounds like Morse code. From my Boy Scout knowledge of Morse, her repeated '.--. .-.' says PR, PR, PR, PR. An obsession with public relations? Possibly. But from what I've seen of her today, she's a pampered moggy asleep in the sun. The gentleman to my left is a 'slick dude' in a midnight black suit, crisp white shirt and diamond cufflinks. He looks like the office superspy, able to leap from buildings and land without so much as a ruffled hair. His aura of invincibility tells me he must work in Sales. I look at his pen. As I suspected: 'Ball. *Roller*ball.' Able to write at speeds faster than the human eye can detect, it can conceal poison darts, small nuclear warheads and an after dinner toothpick. Best not to mess with this guy. Further along the table is a man in an indigo shirt and a loosely fitting yellow tie. He's writing onto a sketchbook using a chisel-tipped marker pen. It's one used by artists, which looks good in the shop but has a nasty habit of bleeding through paper when used. What's the bet that there will be numerous doodles left on the table at the end of the meeting? This graffiti artist must work in Advertising.

Oh, hang on. I'm needed.

"Pardon, what was the question?"

"Would doing things yesterday, that we'd planned to do tomorrow, make us more efficient today?"

"No. How can we act in the past?"

"Thanks for your input, *Writer.*"

Apologies for the distraction. HOD knows of my reluctance for change, and was seeking my buy-in to his plan. As long as I keep nodding and smiling, I should be able to avoid further questions and keep writing these words. Back to my assessment of the pens and their owners.

Next to the advertising executive is a gaunt-looking man in a grey suit who's sitting behind a leather folio containing two pads of paper, a small calculator and a twelve-inch ruler with the word 'Precision' stamped onto it. He's hunched over the desk with his head six inches from the pads, writing with one of those architect-style technical pens that has a tip so fine that it could be used to write a thesis on the back of a postage stamp. I guess he's either an accountant or someone with an unnatural attention to detail. Maybe a consultant brought in to build a one-handled wheelbarrow? I've gone cold at the thought of this, but it's nothing compared to the nervous tick, or rather 'Bic', that I've developed from the presence of six stationery cupboard biros that are scribbling away to my right.

Writing with a biro is the emotional equivalent of giving your loved one a plastic rose on Valentine's Day. It shows disregard for the beauty, craft and tradition of writing. How can an art, once performed by monastic scribes, have degenerated into little more than creative candyfloss? I'd rather scratch a stick in the sand than write with something with a 'dead' nib, that weighs too little and rattles as I write. To me, biros represent the throwaway culture of modern society, which exists on microwave ready-meals and instant coffee. Life is about quality, not quantity, of experience. Hence why I'm writing this with a beautifully balanced, gold-nibbed, vintage fountain pen.

I am the twelfth person at the meeting. The twelfth man. The one with a conscience. My pen is a 1951 Mabie Todd. It is green marbled, gold trimmed and has a

'No. 2' fine nib. It is a Swan, 'The Pen of the British Empire', though I call it 'Old George' in respect for the king who was still alive when the pen was made. I do have newer fountain pens, such as a Parker Sonnet and Duofold, but use older pens when I want to make a statement. (I steer clear of Montblanc as they look like Frosty the Snowman once used them to dislodge something from his nose.) Making a statement is important to me as a writer. If I want greater effect, then I'll bring out a bottle of ink during a meeting, unscrew the top and leave both on the table for a while. I'll watch for responses from my colleagues as I hold the pen over the open bottle and toggle the filler lever. (The trick is to wince like you're about to push the pen into an electric plug socket. If you want to go one better, make a high-pitched whining noise as well and then pass the pen and bottle to the person next to you, while shaking your head and asking if they could 'do the honours'.)

I take great pride in using fountain pens. They represent craftsmanship and a love of writing. What else, other than an artist's brush, can transmit the voice of the soul so beautifully? Vintage fountain pens, especially, have the history that makes a writer like me go weak at the knuckles. One only has to stop and think about all the stories they've written. A pen that has clocked up a million words, a lifetime's memories, has greater value to me than the most expensive piece in a jeweller's window. And it has personality: idiosyncrasies that make it unique. For example, I know that a right-handed person once owned Old George. I can tell this by the way the nib is worn on the right side.

To a right-hander, this would be barely noticeable. But to me, a cack-handed leftie, it makes the pen write in a scratchy, splatty fashion as I push its point along the paper.

My love of old fountain pens has developed since childhood. First there was 'Old Scratchy', a Mabie Todd Blackbird that I found in a lift-top desk at primary school. Then there was 'Bard the Impossible', a horrible thing that kept clogging and was eventually thrown out of a college window while writing an essay about Macbeth. 'Little Squirter', a Parker Slimfold, was given to me by Mrs H after she said it reminded her of me. Then there's 'Wetsock William', the one with the leaky bladder, which I keep close to the blotter. All of these pens were, or are, special to me. None are perfect, but an old pen doesn't need to be in mint condition. That they have been used and loved is what counts. So as I look around this meeting room at the half-chewed biros, the clicking pencil, slick rollerball, chunky marker, delicate draughter and weighty baton, I know that my pen is the one that's most loved and has the most secure future. Fountain pens are built to endure. They are a statement of the perpetuity of tradition. Forevermore. Everlasti-

Oh, curses. I've run out of ink.

Stop – Unplug – Escape – Enjoy

Which is your favourite pen,
and what is its name?

March

VII

THE MAGIC WITHIN

My observations this year have, I believe, focused too much on the activities of other people. I'm not normally so obsessed by the postwoman's bundle (okay, perhaps I am) or how we 'stamp' our identity at work. It's time to slow things down by spending a day doing something quiet, simple and relaxing. I'm going to enjoy some time in the kitchen. Not cooking, but following recipes of a different kind. I'm going to make some writing ink.

Fountain pens may be beautiful, joyous things, but it's the ink within them that's most special. I'm not talking about cartridge ink, which is the writing equivalent of drinking champagne through a plastic straw, or biro ink, which smells like a disposable carrier bag. I'm talking about proper ink that comes in a bottle, can be swirled like brandy in a glass and which smells like apple blossom after rain.

If a pen can communicate our thoughts, dreams, and emotions and be the voice of our soul, then ink is the medium that carries the message. As Ekhart Tolle suggests, "All true artists, whether they know it or not, create from a place of no-mind, from inner stillness". Writing ink, therefore, is the magic that allows nothing to become something. It catches the fleeting idea and seeks out the glances of those who wish to see. Even a random ink splat will mean something to someone.

Shop-bought ink provides us with choice. Choice of colour, permanence, scent and fluidity. But we writers can go one further. Inks can be *blended*. They can also be made using natural dyes that have extra meaning. Which is what I'm going to do today. But first, I'm going to tell you why writing ink is so special to me.

Over the past twenty-five years I've (literally) messed with all sorts of writing inks. I started at school by cutting open ink cartridges of different colours and pouring them into a beaker. At first I was looking to create a colour that I called 'Slate Blue'. I mixed blue ink with the smallest amount of black until I had something 'subdued and refined'. Not the blue-black ink used by headmasters and people of superior standing, but something more down-to-earth and organic.

I discovered my love of antique books at the age of 14. Many of them had semi-faded copperplate inscriptions – lovely bronzed writing in various tints of sepia. This began a quest to blend the perfect sepia-coloured ink. Early attempts resulted in a 'flat brown' that lacked the desired richness of tone and reminded me of the ink in a felt-tip pen. Then I added different shades of red (cherry red was especially good) and the odd drop of blue, until I had bronze ink with a wash of port-like burgundy running through it. This looked blood red in the bottle, but which darkened to the desired colour on the page. Perfect. Well, nearly.

Ink, when blended to a unique colour, has personality. But it lacks soul. It needs a few drops of sentiment to make it come alive and have extra meaning. Sentiments, as I have found, can be harvested from wherever our memories are fondest. As a countryman who loves waterside places, I've found these places to be the rivers and lakes I've fished over the years. It only takes a drop or two of filtered lake or river water for a bottle of ink to suddenly have extra meaning. So if you receive a letter from me, run your fingers over the words and know that you've made contact with some of the best and most famous lakes and rivers in the UK. They've 'literally' flowed onto the paper before you.

Blending inks of different colours is not, of course, making them from scratch. But it's a good way to start, creating something that will quickly enhance your enjoyment of writing. Making inks is a different craft, with seemingly endless possibilities.

My interest in making ink from raw ingredients began when I discovered a book in a bric-a-brac shop. It was entitled 'A Booke of Secrets, 1596'. (Or, more accurately, *A Booke of Secrets: Shewing divers waies to make and prepare all sorts of Inke, and Colours... necessarie to be knowne of all Scriveners, Painters, and others that delight in such Arts*'.) It described ways of making inks from wine, beer, brandy, oak galls, hazelnuts, vitriol (ferrous sulphate, traditionally made from rusty nails) and lampblack (candle soot). It was the closest thing to a book on alchemy that I'd ever seen. I purchased it and hurried home. That was many years ago. Since then I've recreated the historic inks mentioned in the book, I've experimented with different ingredients and have furthered my reading. I've learned that there are four main types of ink that can be created without the assistance of a chemistry set or reinforced underpants. Each follows a basic formula: colorant; liquid (usually distilled water or rainwater, or beer or wine if you want the ink to stick better to the paper); stabiliser to prevent the ingredients from separating (gum arabic is best; it can be purchased in crystal, powder, or liquid form from art shops); a colour preserver (white vinegar) and a preservative (salt). All these inks are best suited to a dip pen or quill, as they tend to clog or corrode a fountain pen.

Firstly there is Iron Gall Ink. This dark purple-brown ink is made from oak galls, also known as oak apples. (These are swellings that appear on the buds or leaves of oak trees. They grow to a rounded shape, up to two inches in diameter, due to a little wasp grub that lives inside them. Wait until you see a little hole drilled through the shell of the gall, which indicates that the wasp has flown free, and then harvest and dry the galls for future use.)

Recipe: Take several dried galls (the number depends upon their size and the amount of ink you want to make; four galls would be the minimum) crush or chop them into quarters and add them to a saucepan with either rusty nails or rusty wire wool added (this is needed for the chemical reaction between the vitriol and the tannic acid in the galls). Cover with distilled water and leave for three days. Then remove any scum from the surface of the water and bring the remainder to the boil. Boil gently for an hour, stirring occasionally. Try the ink on some paper for colour and consistency. If it's too light or too runny, then continue boiling. Strain the contents through a muslin cloth placed over a colander, stir in half a tablespoon of vinegar and half a tablespoon of salt, then store in a sealed glass jar at room temperature. (You can omit the vinegar and salt, and the ink will continue to mature over several weeks, becoming darker, but with risk of mould forming.)

Secondly there is Walnut Ink. Make a large batch, as it's by far the nicest to write with. Use rubber gloves and wear old clothes or an apron, as walnut is a strong dye.

Recipe: Take 20 walnut husks (the green, fleshy part on the outside of the hard shell. Collect them as they fall from the tree). Cut or smash the husks into quarters. Add the husks to a saucepan (as before, with rusty nails or wire wool added as this will make the ink darker). Cover them with water, wine or beer; add a teaspoon of gum arabic (optional) and boil for an hour. Remove from the heat and leave to soak in the saucepan for up to a week (the longer the soaking, the stronger the ink). Strain the husks from the ink, add half a tablespoon of vinegar, half a tablespoon of salt and stir until the salt dissolves. The ink can be stored in a sealed glass jar at room temperature.

Thirdly there is Berry or Root Ink. This can be made from those fruits and roots that might stain the cuffs of an eager forager. Berries such as elderberry and blackberry make purplish-blue ink; strawberries and raspberries make pinkish-red ink, beetroot makes a strong red ink. Other berries, such as haws, sloes, cherries and damsons can be used but lack the intensity of colour of those listed earlier. They can, however, be added to other berries to change the colour and give seasonal variation. I've found the best roots to be dandelion (makes brown ink), meadow sweet (makes dark brown/black ink), carrots (orange ink) and nettle (yellowish-brown ink). (As an aside, alder bark – though neither a berry or root – makes strong red-orange ink, and all parts of the eucalyptus tree make excellent scented ink in shades of deep rusty-red to orangey-brown and green. You'll need to pulp them, and be sure to use gloves to avoid staining your hands.)

Recipe: Put a cup of berries or finely-chopped roots into a metal sieve placed over a bowl. Push and 'scrub' them against the mesh of the sieve with the back of a spoon so that the juice drips into the bowl below. When there's no more juice to squeeze out, add half a tablespoon of vinegar and half a tablespoon of salt to the juice in the bowl. Stir until the salt dissolves. You may wish to strain this mixture through a muslin cloth, but it's not essential. Add half a teaspoon of gum arabic if the ink is too runny, or add more water if it's too thick. Don't be tempted to boil the mixture, as you'll end up with a sticky jam. Store the ink in a sealed glass jar in the fridge and it will keep for several weeks.

Fourthly there is Roman Ink (also known as Lampblack Ink) – the most popular ink used by calligraphers as it never fades and doesn't eat into paper or parchment like ferrous inks. Lampblack is the waxy soot traditionally found near the wick of an oil lamp, but burning candles or wood also produces it. I've found that the best way to create lampblack is to hold a metal spoon in the smoke of a burning candle and watch the soot build. Let the spoon cool and then scrape off the soot, which will have a lovely waxy texture that makes for thick dark ink. As I like my inks to have sentimental provenance, I also use the sooty build-up from the chimney of my Kelly Kettle and from the underside of my campfire frying pan. There are two recipes for Roman Ink. The first is quick and easy; the second is for purists.

Easy recipe: Place five teaspoons of lampblack into a metal or glass bowl; add hot distilled water one drop at a time to the lampblack, which usually floats at first, and stir until you have an inky black liquid; add 1-2 teaspoons of gum arabic (amount depends upon the thickness of ink that you require) and stir. The ink can be used straightaway or stored in a sealed glass jar at room temperature.

Purist's recipe: Add gum Arabic crystals to a mortar and pestle and pound until they become a fine powder; add distilled water until a syrup is formed that's thick enough to coat your fingertip; add lampblack to the mixture, a bit at a time, stirring with the pestle until you have a tar-like paste. This can take an hour. Then really grind the mixture in the mortar until the mixture is smooth. You will then have a treacly paste that can be stored in a jar. To make it into ink, remove a tablespoon of paste and place into a separate jar. Add distilled water and stir until you have the desired consistency.

There you have it: an indispensable guide to making writing inks. I never thought I'd write something that resembles a cookbook, but it's been the easiest way to describe the inks I'll be making today. However, there's magic to be added to each recipe – a message to be carried in your ink. When your ink's been made, at the point when you're about to pour it into the glass storage jar, pause for a moment and say the following words:

"All are different, no two the same.
What was, still is
And will be so again."

That's the spell that locks in the magic. Let your writing release it.

April

VIII

A NEW WRITING DESK

It's pleasing how one's creative time helps to prepare us for whatever tasks and challenges the day will present. My day was spent making ink. My task now is to begin writing with it. But I need some support to do this. Fortunately for me, it has arrived in the form of twenty-nine pieces of wood, three legs and six handles. All thanks to my friend Bryan.

Bryan contacted me recently, informing me that he was downsizing his home. He had, he said, a 'spare' writing desk (oh, the luxury of having *two* writing desks). If I could collect it, then it would be mine. So I went to Bryan's house to collect my gift.

Bryan welcomed me to his home and walked me through to his study. "Here's the desk," he said, "sixty-four inches wide and forty-eight inches deep, made from hardwood with an attractive teak veneer." He paused, and then said: "You're not going to lift it on your own, are you?" A test lift of one corner proved that I was not.

I returned the following day with my father and uncle. With Bryan's help we were able to lift the desk into the back of a hired van and transport it to my cottage. Here, with the six drawers removed, we were able to shunt and slide the desk up the stairs and into my study.

All was not well. While pushing the desk into position in my writing room, my uncle said, "'Ere, it's got a wobble!" A quick look underneath showed that the desk was missing a leg. He continued, "It must 'av snapped off when we slid it up the stairs". Sure enough, there was the leg at the bottom of the stairs, looking like a puppy that had missed its morning walk. "Not to worry," I replied, "at least we've got the desk in place."

I thanked my father and uncle, who left rubbing their backs and knees. I returned to the study to inspect my new desk. It was marvellous. My first *proper* writing desk. I gazed at it and imagined all the letters, journals and books that would be written upon its surface.

But, by 'eck, it was big. The desk was taking up two-thirds of the available space in the room (the rest was filled by my bookcase and an old electric fire that no longer produces heat but which glows with a mock flame and makes a pleasant whirring noise). With all this in place, I'd barely be able to fit into the room.

My challenge for today, therefore, is to make an impromptu leg for the desk, find a chair small enough to fit between the desk and the wall, and fill the desk's drawers with pens, writing paper and special things that assist the creative process (like my secret bottle of port that will be stashed at the back of the largest drawer for those late-night writing sessions).

To work then: first, the table leg. I've decided to be ultra-inventive and use a stack of old books to prop up the desk. Nobody's ever done that before, right? But what choice of books? Should I choose spiritual and

A NEW WRITING DESK

inspirational tomes, upon which my future books will be written? Or should I use the shelf-fillers that were given to me as presents but which I had absolutely no intention of reading? Naturally, I've chosen the latter. Soon the desk will be supported by six of the fattest (or should I say 'densest'?) books I could find: *Cubist Architecture of the 20th Century*; *Pesticides and their Place in Modern Agriculture*; *Economics for Dummies*; *A Clubber's Guide to Ibiza*; *The Fashion of Jean Paul Gaultier*; and *French for Beginners*. A beer mat will top the stack, removing the last wobble from the table and giving the pile some literary credibility.

Second job: the chair. I've measured the gap between desk and wall. Seventeen inches: too narrow for a leather director's chair. That dream will have to wait. Mrs H popped in and suggested I use a beanbag. But the thought of shuffling my buttocks on warm balls caused me to clench my cheeks and go pale. It would have to be the farmhouse chair from the kitchen. I've always liked that chair. Its legs are lathed like the stair banisters of this cottage, so it's a chair at home in its surroundings. I've fetched it from the kitchen and offered it into the space. It fits. Just. With a squeeze and gymnastic leg movement that would make John Cleese proud, I'll be able to lift and then slide myself into the space between chair and desk.

Ahh. My desk; my new writing chair. My new place of creativity, inspiration and quiet tipple.

I'll open the drawers of the desk and carefully position my stationery. Fountain pens will go into the top drawer, writing paper and envelopes into the second, notepads and books into the third. ("Only writing pads in there Dear, no booze whatsoever...") The remaining three drawers will become home to dozens of notebooks, all filled with my scribbly writing and sketches made during my travels. Some contain photos; others have leaves and flowers pressed between their pages. A lifetime of nature observation contained in just three drawers? I don't know if this is good or bad? It makes me yearn to be outside, extending my knowledge.

And when I'm done I'll sit at the desk, pondering its future. Soon it will be cluttered with all manner of souvenirs collected from the woods and fields. There will be acorns, pinecones, pebbles and eggshells. By winter it will have a well-burned candle oozing onto its surface; there will be tea stains, ink splats and scratches visible in the few areas of the desk not covered by paper and books. Like a well-travelled suitcase, it will bear the stamps and scuffs of adventure. But for now, the desk is an open expanse of teak waiting for the first sheet of paper to be placed ceremoniously upon its surface.

And so, in real time, I take a fountain pen from the top drawer, remove its lid and study its nib, picturing how the ink will flow and create lines that have meaning. Paper will be next, held up to the light to reveal textures hidden from first sight. But will it be enough? I need something extra, something that will tell the world that I'm a writer.

Time, I think, to go shopping.

May

IX

TYPE, WRITER

There's something irresistible about antique shops, bric-a-brac fairs, jumble sales, car boot sales and house clearances that attracts the dyed-in-the-wool bargain hunter. It's like being a heron flying over a pond full of caviar-flavoured goldfish. All it takes is a sign saying 'second-hand' for the individual to reach into his or her pockets to see how much cash they're carrying. This is how I came to be in a bric-a-brac shop today.

Mrs H and I were shopping in the Cotswold town of Cirencester. We'd visited a gentleman's outfitters, enjoyed lunch at a pie shop and looked at ladies' fashions in shops with bright lights. Everything was going to plan until the prospect of visiting a shop filled with stilettos proved too much for me to bear.

"Sweetheart," I said, "I'm going to look over there; see you in a minute."

I left Mrs H to her footwear indulgence and headed across the market square to a row of boutique shops. One of them specialised in antiques and curios. From what I could see in the window it stocked everything from old coins to authentic Second World War uniforms.

Ooooh. *Tingle. Tingle tingle. Thumpety thump.* It wouldn't do any harm to have a quick look, would it?

The second-hand shop turned out to be a labyrinth of interconnected rooms, each selling a different type of treasure. There were areas that showcased cutlery and crockery, others displayed cut glass, gardening tools, books, furniture, in fact anything and everything to furnish a traditionalist's home. It was a shop that knew and understood its customers who, like me, didn't want to find things easily. They wanted to rummage and make chance discoveries. Vinyl records were displayed alongside old army boots; an antique wardrobe was filled with teddy bears; a bowler hat was resting upon the head of a rocking horse, and a fishing creel held an assortment of Bakelite doorknobs. It was my sort of place. Inviting, mysterious, inexpensive.

I worked my way from one room to the next, surveying the contents as quickly as possible in case there was an absolute 'steal' to be found. There were many. A pair of wooden candlesticks caught my eye, then a cut glass decanter, then a garden trowel. But I kept my hands in my pockets. The well-trained bargain hunter always believes that there could be something better around the corner. He or she only picks something up if the item and price tag are right. Which is what finally happened when I opened the lid of a wicker laundry basket and found a gleaming typewriter inside. It was a Corona No. 3 with polished workings and enamelled casing. The keys were worn but usable. It looked as if it had come straight from the study of a great writer. Someone of learning, who had used this machine to type a modern classic, while knowing that it was a thing of beauty – a dream to use and something that told the world of the writer's refined taste and literary standing. I had to have it. I looked at the price tag. Fifteen pounds. Was that all? Surely the price was missing a zero? It was such a bargain. A real bargain. And, in case you'd missed the message: it was a total and utter bargain. Yet how could I approach the shopkeeper who'd apparently under-priced the item? I'd look like a teenage boy requesting an under-counter copy of *Melons Monthly* from his newsagent. I knew the solution. I'd get Mrs H to buy it.

I exited the shop and ran over to my beloved, who was waiting for me in the middle of the market square.

"Babe, you've got to come and see this. This amazing, perfect, stunning thing. I…I…need you to buy it for me."

"I see," she replied. "Like the time you got me to buy that rusty primus stove on FleaBay. The one you said would make our camping trips perfect but which wheezed, farted and squealed like an orgasmic wart hog every time we used it?"

"This is different. It's such a bargain. It's just what I need to write 'the' book. And it would look sooo good in my study."

"What, between the dried-up oil lamp and that lump of driftwood that's supposed to 'have meaning' but which smells like King Lear's codpiece?"

"No, no. This is better. I *neeeed* to have it."

"So, what is it?"

"Come and see."

I walked Mrs H to the shop, through the door, past the shopkeeper and to the alcove with the wicker basket.

I removed the lid and lifted out the vintage typewriter.

"Here. Isn't it beautiful?"

"It's a typewriter."

"Yes."

"An old typewriter."

"Yes."

"That's missing the A, B and N keys."

"Oh. What? Well that doesn't matter."

"What if you want to write an article about a banana?"

"Well I don't. I want to buy this typewriter. Before someone else buys it and we have to leave the shop knowing that we could have bought a bargain but instead we missed out and have to go and look for another one exactly like this and at the same price and that will take ages and..."

"Okay. How much is it."

"Fifteen pounds."

"Oooh. Bargain."

I handed the typewriter to Mrs H and, being the gentleman that I am, picked up her shopping bags and cowered six feet behind her as she approached the shopkeeper.

"My husband wishes to purchase this typewriter," said Mrs H. "He believes that it could aid his creativity."

The shopkeeper looked up from his magazine and raised an eyebrow. He stared in my direction. I needed urgent credibility. With confident swagger I said, "Ah yes; you probably haven't heard of me, but I'm the writer who was called upon by the Government to write leaflets about the safe disposal of agricultural waste plastics. I also penned a national press campaign about planting trees for the Millennium".

"I know your type," he replied. "You're a writer. Always got your head in the clouds dreaming up your next story. I bet you'll write about me someday, twisting the facts to suit whatever angle you've adopted. Well if you do, be kind. Tell everyone that I'm the Cotswold's answer to Mel Gibson, that I drive a Ferrari and that Claudia Schiffer is my girlfriend."

"Sounds reasonable. Do I get a discount?"

"No."

"Okay then Mel, sell me the typewriter and go back to reading your copy of *Patchwork Weekly*."

Mrs H handed over the cash and we left swiftly, half expecting the shopkeeper to chase after us. But he didn't and we made it home, smugly knowing that we'd secured the bargain of the day.

That was earlier today. The typewriter now has pride of place on my writing desk. I've run my fingers over its keys, flicked levers and turned dials. I can push the keys and hear miniature hammers punching the roller. Doing so gives me a feeling of power, as if I'm in control of every letter. Well, every letter except A, B and N. I can open my study window and let the sound of typing inform my neighbours that I'm overflowing with ideas. The village will be buzzing with news that Fennel is working on his latest masterpiece. I will be known for my talent. And all because of this wonderful, beautiful machine that sits on my desk like…oh dear. Like a hunk of polished junk.

Time, I think, to make an escape.

Stop – Unplug – Escape – Enjoy

What item would look great
on your writing desk?

JUNE

X

OUT AND ABOUT
WITH A NOTEBOOK

"Hello? Can you hear me? Hello! Are you there? Fennel here. He of recent typewriter shame. Calling to you from the field. Hello! I'm having an out-of-office experience. Are you there? I need to make contact!"

Damn it, I don't think this thing's working. Best I do it the old-fashioned way and put pen to paper.

Ah, that's better. There you are.

Today I am out and about with my nature notebook. I have my ear to the ground, a nose for a good story and a book full of clichés. I'm looking for dirt. Filth. Things that get wet when they shouldn't, high when they ought to know better, and run when they know they've been spotted.

As a roving reporter, I ought to be 'up' on so many things: the private lives of politicians, the workings of the stock market, the glinting of celebrity smiles and the secrets of their dustbins. All should be on my radar. But they're not, because I'm not interested. What I am interested in, what I write and care about, exists in the slow lane, somewhere between hand-ploughed fields and a pint of real ale. Where natural things are viewed at a natural pace and where life is served with a healthy dash of humour. A so-called vintage existence, anachronistic living made all the more rewarding by holding a raised eyebrow to the absurdities of modern life. To write about this requires me to experience it first-hand, while maintaining a close-rooted connection to natural things. Which means going outdoors to smell the roses and escape the WiFi signal. Which, as you may have guessed, is where I am now.

I'm sitting in a wood, in a welcome shaft of sunlight, smelling the perfume from a dog rose that's growing through a thicket of holly behind me. It's strange, because I don't remember dog roses having a scent. But I know it's there, as my nose is drawn towards it. Maybe it's an imagined scent? Perhaps I want the pink-blushed flowers to be more attractive than they actually are? It could be that I want to sense something more than the obvious?

It is said that an artist's talent lies in being able to paint what he or she sees, even if it's abstractly removed from what's in view. An 'interpretation' of the scene, that brings greater meaning. We writers do this with words, but an artist in the field has one advantage over us: he or she has *equipment.*

I'm writing this with a pen onto a notebook, but an artist is likely to have a portable studio upon which to work. He or she would likely be sitting here on a wooden stool, looking with raised chin at a canvas upon an easel; there would be a folding table with all manner of items placed upon it: wooden boxes full of paints and brushes, a bottle of wine, a glass, a tray of canapés, a candle-powered fondue-set, and a book entitled

How to Look Good and Impress People. Passers-by would consider the artist 'expert' even if the canvas looked like a blind chimpanzee had painted upon it.

Perhaps I ought to set a trend for writers everywhere and pioneer the use of a portable writing bureau? Something made from mahogany, with sliding drawers, brass handles and a drop-down writing surface; carried on wheels and pulled by a small pony? Or maybe a James Bond-style suitcase that folds out to reveal an inkwell, dip pens, drinks decanter, watermarked writing paper, and cufflinks that emit laser beams when we're left facing an impending deadline? Erm. No. Bureaus like that would be way too grand for me, though I could knock something up from an old tea chest, strap it to a wheelbarrow and see if my neighbour's labrador could haul it along. A fun exercise, for sure, but unnecessary. Why? Because I have a writer's rucksack.

I've just removed the rucksack from my back and now realise that it goes some way towards being a portable study. Not only is it functional, it has character that announces me as a writer on the march. It's a 1950s-style mountaineering bag, with leather straps and brass buckles. It has all manner of things hanging from it, strapped to it and falling from it. There's an enamel mug that clunks as I walk, a gentleman's umbrella that rarely gets used, an emergency jumper, some baling twine and a karabiner that, well, I don't know what that's for, and a small Kelly Kettle. I've nicknamed the rucksack 'Old Lunker'. It contains field books for the identification of wildlife and different types of townsfolk; a lunchbox, thermos flask and tea caddy;

a survival knife and compass; a waterproof cushion; a camera and lightweight tripod; and, most importantly, a notebook, pen, bottle of ink, and a pencil.

Although a writer can write with a variety of makeshift tools (I once wrote in mud onto my leg when I had a brilliant idea but no paper or pen) it adds to the enjoyment of writing if one can write onto something special: such as a proper, quality notebook. A leather-bound journal, especially, says a lot about us. It communicates that we love to write, that we take pride in the process and wish to preserve what we've written. It's equivalent to the canvas that the artist takes into the field, because they know that a sketchbook is too run-of-the-mill, too normal, too everyday. Instead, they push the easel out and see what inspiration comes from their palette.

My notebook is not in my rucksack at the moment. It is resting upon my knee as I write these words. It's nice to see it out in the open, completing the scene that I always desire: sitting with my back to a tree, surveying my surroundings, breathing deeply and writing about what I sense and feel. A notebook reserved for outdoor writing is destined to record things as they happen – all the fine detail of adventure that would be forgotten by the time one returns home. Flicking through this notebook (it has an oak-tanned leather cover, with marbled endpapers and cream paper) I can retrace the footsteps of a dozen or more walks experienced since the start of the year. One entry stands out as my favourite. It describes a walk through the same wood as today, when I was here last month. The words appear disjointed, like dabs of paint added quickly, but together they create a picture that's immediate and fresh:

"May 4th – Priory Wood – dawn walk – mist in fields – fox in lane – barn owl over meadow – cowslips, plantains, purple orchids in verges – elder in leaf, gorse in flower – orange tip and pale blue butterflies above hedgerow – cow parsley, ragged robin and goosegrass adjacent to wood – bluebells on woodland floor – hazel leaves furry, beech leaves semi-transparent, ash leaves in cluster – woodpecker tapping for grubs, great tit singing, tree creeper on beech trunk – earth musty, air cool – rested for tea, tasted life – deer came close – silent communion – gave thanks – for everything."

The landscape has changed since then: subtly in some cases, like the opacity of the leaves, and spectacularly in others, like the colour of the woodland floor. Which is why it's important to get out and about with a notebook, to observe things and preserve them before they're gone. So I ask this of you: go for a walk, to see and experience, but mostly to write. As American poet Mary Oliver said, "I have a notebook with me all the time, and I begin scribbling a few words. When things are going well, the walk does not get anywhere; I finally just stop and write." That's good advice. Make time to stop and write, in places that inspire you. Look closely, because the best observations require us to view things – in a certain light.

Stop – Unplug – Escape – Enjoy

What's in your writing bag?
Anything missing?

JULY

XI

CANDLELIGHT

There was a programme on television last night about the workings of the human eye. It explained that our eyes see in two dimensions and that our brain then processes the signals into a three-dimensional image. As babies, we saw and processed things in two dimensions (hence why stark black and white patterns are easiest for newborns to see), and then as we grew up, and our spatial awareness increased, so our brains learned to 'make up the gaps' and present us with a three-dimensional view of the world. Interesting. eh? It does give us some ammunition, doesn't it, for whenever someone – perhaps a critic – calls us 'two-dimensional'? Clearly, they mean no offence. It's just that their brain hasn't properly developed and that they lack spatial awareness. In short, they have the brain of a child. It's up to you whether you tell them this. My advice is to keep on writing regardless.

The TV programme did, however, make me think. If our brain processes and 'fills in the gaps' based upon conditioning and experience, then there's an element of us filtering what we choose to see. If our eyes saw everything, then there'd be little left for imagination. One's vision, therefore, is rather selective based upon the mood we're in and what we choose to observe. It's like viewing a darkened scene with either a halogen lamp or a lighted candle. One shines brightly and illuminates everything; the other is duller and casts a faint glow onto its surroundings. One cuts through the darkness; the other mingles with the shadows. Which one would we choose to light our path? It depends upon where we are, where we're going, and how keen we are to get lost. Losing ourselves can, amidst the panic, trigger intense creativity.

Halogen bulbs are great for car headlights, but I wouldn't want one shining on my writing desk. Which is why I'm writing this by candlelight. The gold nib of my pen is reflecting the yellow flame and the page is bathed in an orange glow that flickers, fades and swirls, as if reacting to whatever I'm writing. It pleases me that a candle produces such a natural light, especially when we consider 'Energy Saving' alternatives. Light Emitting Diode? If light was meant to be 'ice blue' then God would have turned the sun down at bit, don't you think? And light without heat? No thank you. I enjoy the warmth of a candle glow.

Nearly all of my writing is done by candlelight. I enjoy the ritual of selecting a candle to suit my mood (beeswax church candles are my favourite), then striking a match, lighting the wick and placing the candle into a glass jar or onto a candleholder. I'll then sit back to breathe in the smell of sulphur from the match smoke and fumes from the candle. I'll choose which fountain pen and ink colour suits my mood, then I'll open my leather folio and begin writing.

CANDLELIGHT

Writing by candlelight is recommended. It pulls at our ancestral strings, reminding us of when early man drew upon the walls of his cave. Candles, therefore, have a timeless quality (even though, as they burn down, they present a very accurate measure of time). A candle flame can transfix us for hours; we can stare at the blues and purples at its base, and watch them rising into yellows and oranges at the tip; they twist and roll, and beneath them, wax oozes against the heat. It's an act of silent, sensory meditation. A ceremonial act; no wonder they're used in prayer.

Many of the candles we use today are mass-produced, made from a mixture of paraffin wax and beeswax. Some are even made from soybean wax. (Paraffin wax is cheaper, burns brightest and without an odour; beeswax candles burn slower and have a marked scent, which is reminiscent of old churches.) You can still get traditional, handmade candles (hand-dipped taper candles are excellent) but the true connoisseur will make his or her own. It's so easy. Just take two saucepans (assembled one atop the other, bain-marie style), some wax granules, a wick and a mould, then simply melt the wax and pour into the mould to cool. I have candles set in old jam jars; some have petals and pieces of pipe tobacco sprinkled into them; others are dyed with coloured wax to match my writing inks. And, of course, I have candles made from the nubs of old candles, meaning that their flame never truly goes out.

A supply of unique candles can be made quickly and relatively cheaply. It's a rewarding hobby, where the candle maker has the added benefit of being able to call him- or herself an Artisan Chandler. But we could go one further: owning a beehive and being able to make home-grown beeswax candles. What a lovely provenance: that the bees that have fed upon the flowers in our garden and provided us with honey, could also provide the wax for our candles. Every year's batch would be subtly different, scented by the flowers that bloomed brightest. How cherished those candles would be. How organic. How personal. How meaningful. So much harvesting of energy, released as a flame during our time at the writing desk.

Of course, you could choose to be uber-traditional and make authentic 13th Century 'Tallow Candles' from animal fat. All you'd need is a block of lard, a wick and a lighted match, and you'd be in business. It's not advisable though, as you're likely to fill your home with foul-smelling black smoke that would permeate your clothes, carpets and furniture and stay in your house for years. I know. I've done it, and even though I've moved house twice since then, I can still smell it on some of the furniture. (This is why beeswax is associated with church candles. The wealthy of the parish did not want their 'Sunday Best' garments ruined by acrid 'peasant' smoke, and so the church invested in expensive but cleaner-smelling beeswax candles.)

The best candles I've ever seen were in a tumbledown 17th Century pub in Gloucestershire. I'd travelled there with my college friends to watch the Severn Bore pushing up the river. I soon forgot about the phenomenon once I'd seen the equally impressive candles inside the pub. Each table had upon it a squat, dark green bottle into

CANDLELIGHT

which was thrust a candle. Actually, that's not correct. The candle wasn't so much 'thrust' as melted onto a volcano-like mound of solidified molten wax. Both bottle and table were coated in waxy ooze, which was made up of a variety of red, blue and white colours. I asked the landlord about the candles. "They've been here since the pub began," he replied. "They're as much a part of the place as the timbers above your head. As one candle burns down, we stick another on top. But enjoy them while you can. We've been told they don't meet EU hygiene standards so we've got to switch to varnished tables and put electric lights in the ceiling."

I caressed the lumpy mass of wax around each bottle, feeling layer upon layer of history beneath my hands. Three hundred years of conversations and merriment locked within the strata of wax, and all about to be thrown into a skip because of some European bureaucrat. "Blummin' authoritarian," I thought. "How dare he snuff out our pleasure?" But then, who was I to object? I was merely the oppressed minority, clinging on to tradition. I'd have loved to make a stand, but I'd have needed the help of my female friends. Why? Because women purchase 90% of candles. That makes them the real fire starters, proving they're the ones who've seen the light.

Find and see your light. Lose yourself in the swirling flame. Be warmed by it. Treasure it. Write by it. Let it shine bright and true. While the candle burns, so does your passion.

Believe in the light. It's there to guide you.

Stop – Unplug – Escape – Enjoy

What will you find in 'the flickering' between flame and imagination?

AUGUST

XII

MAKING AN IMPRESSION

Writers are often instructed by their publishers to "write for your audience". But this can lead to mimicking authors already in that space. Better, I feel, for a writer to develop a unique voice and perspective, to attract a distinct and loyal following. As the author and theologian Howard Thurman said, "Follow the grain in your own wood…Don't ask what the world needs. Ask what makes you come alive, and go do it. Because what the world needs is people who have come alive". It's great advice because readers want a glimpse of the author's world, not theirs. Which leads us nicely to discussing what makes you individual, different and special.

A question for you: are you more individual now, with the confidence of years, than you were when younger? Do you 'follow the crowd' or deliberately buck trends? Do you speak up and speak out, or stay schtum? And if this hasn't always been the case, why did you change?

Think back to when you were at school, the place where peer pressure and rules often suppress individuality. If you turned up wearing winkle-picker shoes and a bright pink wig, chances are that your friends would have mocked you, or your teachers would have pulled you out of class. It was best to play safe, and very difficult not to conform. Being individual was not encouraged. You were part of the cloning system designed to produce 'rounded individuals'. How ironic that in later life, 'leaders' are defined by their maverick streak and ability to think differently to others? Yep, if you want to stand out and avoid rolling off the table, you need to be a square marble.

Communicating one's individuality is easy when people can see and hear us. Our choice of clothes, hairstyle, behaviour, even the way we speak, reveals our personality to others. But what if all they know of us is a letter? Scrawls of ink on a piece of paper don't provide much of an opportunity to make a lasting impression. Or do they?

When Beatrix the postwoman delivered the mail this morning, I was so distracted by her radiant beauty that I didn't notice the letter she was carrying in her hand. By the time she'd bent over to slide her goodies though the letterbox, I'd almost fallen out of my hiding place in the garden hedge. But when she'd gone next door, and I'd crept back into the house, I discovered that the letter, not the postwoman, was the most stunningly beautiful thing I'd seen that day.

The letter was not like any other I'd received. It was, to be specific, handmade. Not in a crude Heath Robinson way, rather it was most skilfully crafted, and completely unique. The texture of the envelope resembled that of an old bank note; the sort that gets left in a pocket and ends up being put through the washing machine. It was sturdy but crinkly, and had within it many specks and fibres of something dark and woody. I thought at first that these marks were tea leaves, but on closer inspection realised that they were not. No colour had seeped from them into the paper. The writing on the envelope was a 'scratchy copperplate': beautifully written with a fine-lined pen, but with a slightly shaky hand. I imagined it to have been written by someone either very old, or very cold. The ink was most unusual of all. A greyish amber colour, not especially vibrant, that seemed ghostly in appearance. I drew the envelope closer to my eyes, keen to study it in more detail. And then I noticed the delightful scent. Not a fancy perfume, but instead something rich and earthy. The ink smelled faintly of wood smoke, and the envelope of vanilla. And there was something else. Brandy? Rum? A mixture of both? The letter smelled like Christmas pudding warming in front of a log fire.

The letter inside the envelope was written in the same ink, and on matching paper. It bore an elaborate letterhead, letterpress printed, stating the sender's name and address. To the left of the address was a pen and ink illustration of smoke rising from a decoratively carved pipe, and at the bottom of the page was a small embossing of an oak leaf. The letter was from someone named Brian Holmes. I didn't know him, but he knew me. His letterhead informed me that he was "The Bearded Pipe Puffer of Weston-Super-Mare". This caused me to do a double take. Was it he who had the beard, or the pipe? And was he talking of the smoking variety or the one found in a man's trousers? Brian clearly had a rude sense of humour in addition to his fine taste in stationery.

Sure enough, once I began reading Brian's letter, I knew that he was someone with a keen wit. "Excuse the address, young Fennel," he began, "but one has to be upfront about one's persuasions. I am a lover of pipes, you see, especially big pipes: the sort that cause one's jaw to ache and one's eyes to water. Not everyone can handle one. But I can. I am, after all, an expert puffer!" And then Brian explained that, in addition to his love of pipe-smoking, he was also a connoisseur of quality stationery, making everything himself. "Hope you like the paper. It's made from a mix of cotton, starch, white vinegar, and pulp from old newspapers. And, of course, I've sprinkled in some tobacco leaves from my pipe for good measure." (So that's what the brown flecks were in the paper.) "They're a Caribbean blend, vanilla scented and soaked in rum for extra richness. The ink's a bit special, too. I use the ash from my pipe, mix it with my favourite brandy liquor and add some powdered gum arabic and salt. Clogs up a fountain pen, but is perfect for my old dip pen. Takes a while to write a letter this way, but the process of creation begins way before one starts writing, does it not?"

Brian's words caused me to think about, and redesign, my own stationery. The off-the-shelf stuff was no longer good enough. Something without a bespoke letterhead was too boring. I needed to make an impression. And so it was that I remembered a little venture I began in the nineties.

In 1997, when I was not long out of college, I started a little business making bespoke stationery. I produced letterheads, envelopes and calling cards, usually as one-offs, on quality paper, each bearing an illustration of mine (usually of a game bird, animal, or fish). It was a nice occupation, little more than a hobby, but it helped to fund the purchase of a pen or two.

Alas, my venture was short-lived. Family circumstances dictated otherwise. I had to focus my attentions elsewhere. The business was shut down and my dream of sending beautifully produced letters was put on hold. But now, after receiving today's letter, I'm going to rekindle that dream and begin thinking about how I can improve the look and feel of the letters I send. I think, given that I'm an outdoorsman, I should make seasonal writing paper that includes blossom in spring and leaves in autumn. My ink colour could match, with a verdant green in spring (perhaps made from meadowgrass and lime leaves) and a burnt umber in autumn (made from walnuts and acorns). I could get a Fennel's Priory embossing stamp for the envelopes, and illustrate each letterhead with a seasonal scene. Given that each letter would most likely be written outdoors, I could include a leaf or smudge of soil or berry juice with each letter. These letters would be grounded in place and time, much like me. Though, of course, I'd be missing the boldness of a 'pipe puffing' reputation. 'Fennel the countryman-writer' would do instead. It would be me on and in the page, capturing the world around me. That ought to make a lasting impression. Something that unleashes the true beauty of the handwritten letter. All I'd need to do is find people who appreciate handwritten letters as much as I do, and write to them.

Personalised stationery is beautiful, but it's nothing without content. Writing is what counts. Sometimes it flows, other times it doesn't. To open the envelope of our creativity, we sometimes need to stay up late and brace ourselves for what follows. Be warned: things can get rather abstract when writing into the early hours, especially when the pressure's on to meet a deadline.

Are you ready? Are you prepared? Are you inspired? If so, let's do it.

August

XIII

THE NIGHT SHIFT

*"All things at rest, and imag'd the still voice.
Of quiet, whispering in the ear of night."*

Dr John Brown

The time for discussion and contemplation is over. The new world begins. The pressure is on. Romanticism is off. Off the agenda, and off the menu. There's no time. No hours to dilly-dally. No luxury of a day to think. I need to get things done. Urgently. Right now. By that, I mean now. Not then. Not whenever. Now!

Oh, I'm procrastinating again. Get on with it Fennel, or you'll never start. Shift into higher gear, then grab a pen and write. Write what you need to write, what you've been asked to write, what you're expected to write. Confront the page that taunts you with its whiteness. Face your enemy and fill it with words. You are bigger and stronger than a piece of paper.

I ought not to be stalling, as I know there's no such thing as writer's block. At least, not as long as we've had plenty of time to think about what we want to write, the angles we want to adopt and the story we want to tell. That doesn't help me now, as I don't have time to think.

I have a self-imposed deadline to meet. Tomorrow I shall be going on holiday with Mrs H, so tonight is my last opportunity to write this chapter for you. I've never missed a deadline before, so I'm not going to be late now. I *will* create something. But I don't know what to write. My head's fuzzy and my eyes can barely focus. It's 2am and I have four hours before my wife and I head to the train station. During that time I need to write this chapter, pack for holiday, get some sleep and eat some breakfast. My vision's getting blurry. I can feel my head beginning to rock. But I'm getting excited. An idea's going to pop in from somewhere, because one's mind is most creative when we're half awake.

Albert Einstein used to do his best thinking at times like this. He'd stack books under the left legs of his desk, write with a metal pen and put a steel tray on the floor to his right. He'd begin working in the middle of the night, when he was tired and exhausted. Eventually he'd fall asleep at his desk and drop his pen, which would then roll down the desk and onto the steel tray below. The 'clang' of the pen hitting the tray would wake him, sustaining what he described as "the Nether Space between asleep and awake". It was when doing this that he came up with his Theory of Relativity.

It's too late in the day for me to understand Relativity, but I'm prepared to give Einstein's theory of Nether Space a go. My desk's propped up and the tray's waiting. And to speed things up, I'm going to turn out the lights. So here goes...

It is perhaps ten minutes since I flicked the light switch and the world disappeared from sight. All was lost in the blackness. But after staring into the void, my eyes have adjusted and I can detect the shape of things. This is not good. I can still see. Eyesight can be so blinding. I need to look beyond the face of things. It is time to peel back the veneer of the obvious and take a peek into the fourth dimension. I'm going to close my eyes and explore the world of the muse that inhabits my mind. What does it show me? That darkness is so revealing. The tiniest sound, the subtlest smell, changes in temperature, the texture of things, all become more apparent when sight is removed. But there's more. The 'dead of night' is a lie. When all is silent, and all is dark, the pulse of emotion quickens and a kaleidoscope of imagination flares up. It is when we can reach beyond the plane of the obvious to connect with The Unseen.

Sounds far-fetched? It works, I assure you. Because it's working now.

I could, for example, walk outside right now to lie upon my lawn. Facing up and looking at the stars, I'd stay there until I felt the rumble and spin of the Earth. And when I did, I'd press down into the grass with my fingertips. Why? Because I'd realise that I wasn't static at all, but travelling at a thousand miles per hour as the Earth spins. We are all travelling at this great speed, and without breaking a sweat. It creates gravity, but prevents anything from staying put. No wonder we seek to slow down; we're stuck to the walls of a centrifuge. (Unless, of course, we stand at the North or South Pole and get dizzy.)

A thousand miles per hour? Does knowing this give you a sense of energy? Does it make you want to get up and run to catch that speeding bullet? Or does it make you want to climb out of the catapult? It makes me want to face forward, to see where I'm going. But I can't do this now. It's dark and I'm facing west, so I couldn't see where I'm travelling. But I'm reassured that I'll be at pretty much the same place this time tomorrow. (Only, I hope, asleep in bed while on holiday.) What does this tell me? That those who sprint might travel quicker, but we'll all end up in the same place at the end. We'll all finish with our backs to the ground, facing the same immovable destiny.

How about the speed of light? Or, better still, the *taste* of light? If you could taste sunlight, then would darkness be flavourless? Would it be like chewing mist? Or would darkness be so strong as to overpower our taste buds and get us reaching for a torch to wash out our mouths? Would we keep our mouths closed when walking through shadows, or would we run around, scooping up sunlight and swigging it from cupped hands?

And what if noise could not travel by daylight? Would blue skies make us scream to be heard, and dull days have us covering our ears? Would we be deafened at night, when a raindrop landing on a petal would sound like shattering glass?

Darkness is the mirror into which we must all eventually look. It is the place where we may see our true reflection, were we 'feel' our heartbeat and hear the voice within. My inner voice is talking to me now, asking me questions such as 'why do I allow myself to become busy doing unimportant things for unimportant

THE NIGHT SHIFT

people?' 'Do I believe in time over matter?' 'Does time matter or is matter more important than time?' It's questioning whether time exists, and if so, whether it matters. It's got me thinking: is matter a collection of molecules or the reason why we exist? If there was no time, and nothing mattered, would we bother opening our eyes in the morning? But what if things mattered so much that they created time? Would we exist for the matter, or kill time so that it didn't matter? And what does any of this have to do with writing?

How do you define your reason for living? Surely it's to do that which matters most? The big question, then: "How much does writing matter to you, and your writing matter to others?" For me, writing is my lifeblood. It keeps me true to myself and gives me purpose. It's my tune within. I hear it with, and I hear it without. Without a need. To shout! "Dances in the darkness, echoes in time." Where no one can see me, but all can hear. Words on a page, blindly written? Light to eat, sounds to drink. Food aplenty. All eaten. Words. Written. Upon a page. Each with meaning.

They'll question my words, challenge my dreams. "Aloof," they'll say. Agree with them, I will. "Run," they'll yell. Hide, I will. "Be scared!" they'll threaten. "Have courage," I'll pray. "Be bold," I'll say. "Believe," they'll whisper. "I," I'll say. Nothing, they'll say.

Silence.

Brrrrrrrrrrr. Clang.

Ooh. Where was I? Right, where's the light switch? Okay, there it is. Strewth, where am I? Oh yes, there I am: over there, asleep at my desk.

Stop – Unplug – Escape – Enjoy

When do you do your best writing?
Is it in the Netherspace between
awake and asleep?

September

XIV

'DICTIONERY'

Wow. That was a crazy night. Writing until the early hours, committing to paper whatever came into my head and having an out of body – and out of my mind – experience. I didn't bother going to sleep. Instead I wrote the chapter up into neat and then sat in my garden, re-reading the original scrawl by the light of the rising sun. My thoughts? Hmmm. It's probably the finest fruitcake recipe I'd ever read. But I'm glad I didn't temper it with an editor's pen. I didn't have time to sit and mess with it, so it's pretty raw, but the chapter's all the better for it. It was a pouring of creative thinking onto a page that I could feel but not see. Writing blind, but seeing so much. And I met my deadline.

Thomas Edison, like Albert Einstein, was famous for using the power of sleep to aid innovation. He kept a notepad under his pillow and asked impossible questions to himself when he went to bed. Often he would wake in the middle of the night with the answer to his question, then scribble it down for reference in the morning. This is one of the most powerful techniques for creative writing. I've practiced it for twenty years. It works; though make sure the notebook isn't too chunky, else you'll end up with a cricked neck.

Edison made three revolutionary inventions: the electric light bulb, the phonograph (for recording sound), and a way of recording motion pictures. He also held the patents to over a thousand inventions and pioneered the concept of teamwork to aid creativity. He's the man quoted with saying, "Being busy does not always mean real work. The object of all work is production or accomplishment and to either of these ends there must be forethought, system, planning, intelligence and honest purpose, as well as perspiration. Seeming to do is not doing". Valuable advice for the aspiring writer. If it doesn't work, apply his other quote, "There are no rules here – we're trying to accomplish something". The latter is something I wrote on a piece of card and now keep pinned to the wall above my desk.

I included the Edison quotes partly to help me make a point, and partly to flex my puny academic muscles. I needed to do it because I'm being completely upstaged by a neckless wonder sitting opposite me. Let me explain.

I'm sitting in a train with Mrs H, rattle-tattling along on our way up north. We've just settled down after moving from our original carriage because it was crowded, noisy and smelled like an old shoe. We chanced our arm and snuck into First Class, where we have been hiding for ten minutes. It's a luxuriously quiet, spacious and stench-free carriage. We've each been given a complimentary newspaper from a steward called Claude, and will soon be sipping tea from china cups. Heavenly. Well, it should be. It's First Class. But things are not entirely quiet. There's a chinless, pinstriped

'DICTIONERY'

'banker' sitting opposite us who has, we fear, rumbled our stowaway intentions. But instead of reporting us to the steward, he is doing his best to highlight our 'lower class' tickets. How? By intimidating us with a display of impressive vocabulary.

Walter Big-Head, (as Mrs H has named him) is doing the crossword in one of those broadsheets that are awkward to hold but great for covering the floor when you're sweeping the chimney. He's making a point of muttering the questions under his breath and then, while raising both eyebrows, stares at us as he announces the answer. From the way his lips are moving (it looks like he's suckling a shrew) he's aware of his superior knowledge and wishes to force us into a second-class retreat. We've received several subtle comments, such as, "Hmm. Eight down. 'Cause of staring.' Eight letters, ending in D. Ah yes. *Gapeseed*; Ooh, fourteen across, 'One who lives like a gypsy but is not a true Romany.' Seven letters, second letter I. Ah yes. *Didicoy*." And then, as he stared towards my beloved, "Nine across. 'Flightless bird with flat breastbone.' Six letters, ending in E. *Ratite*. So appropriate..."

Right. We can play this game.

"Rear end, four letters, beginning in A," I say. And another: "To pierce with a needle. Five letters, beginning in P". And how about: "Man who flips pancakes. Six letters, beginning in T". Mrs H has joined my retaliation with a rather witty: "Door without a handle. Eight letters, beginning in K".

That seems to have done the trick. He's folded his newspaper, got up and moved further down the carriage.

Priory United 1 – Pinstripe Academicals 0.

The English language is so rich and varied, yet I have only a moderate vocabulary for a writer. Until recently I thought that 'dicacity' was the art of pleasing lots of urban girlfriends and 'bosselated' was how a line manager feels when he or she meets their targets. Unusual words might sound clever, but they're not as powerful as Plain English and a good point. The gentleman who was sitting opposite us seemed to have swallowed a dictionary, but he'd be the last person we'd invite to a dinner party. So what use was his knowledge? A quickly completed crossword, yes, but his skills are redundant when no one gives a damn.

The study of language, especially the origins of language, most definitely benefits the writer. With so many words going out of fashion, and so many youngsters inventing their own language (A M8 1 A P B4 T?) it would be rather entertaining to resurrect some of the now defunct words in our language and, literally, breathe life into them.

If you've not read it, try getting hold of the book called *Lobcocks and Fartleberries*. Written in 1785 and still in print, it provides a guide to 18th Century slang. My favourites are 'Betwattled' (surprised or confounded), 'Bumfiddle' (one's backside), 'Fambles' (hands), 'Gollumpus' (a large clumsy fellow), 'Hobbledygee' (a pace between a walk and a run), 'Inexpressibles' (breeches), 'Kickerapoo' (dead), 'Mopsqueezer' (housemaid), 'Shabbaroon' (an ill-dressed fellow) and 'Timber Toe' (man with a wooden leg). There are funnier ones, but they are too vulgar to repeat here.

'DICTIONERY'

Maybe we should invent a language of our own by taking the above examples, mixing them with Dickensian slang and adding some Stanley Unwin gobbledegook? It would be fun. But for now, my writing is done. It's time for me to sleep. This train journey will last for several hours, so I will up my footsy toes, pin 'ole my eyesy lids, cup me fambles and dreamo of impossibo languioles.

Ahhh. Here we go. Floaty, snoozy, dreamyville.

Stop – Unplug – Escape – Enjoy

What is your favourite word and why?

October

XV

AWAY FROM IT ALL

> *"I do not indeed know any tract of country in which, within so narrow a compass, may be found an equal variety in the influences of light and shadow upon the sublime or beautiful features of the landscape."*
>
> William Wordsworth

The English Lake District is popular with ramblers, poets, artists, tourists and a young writer named Fennel who seeks somewhere quiet for his autumn holiday. I come here every November, when the peak-season crowds have departed and the mountains and valleys recover their calm. Mrs H first brought me here in 2004, when she became aware that I needed some space to lay myself out, so that I could decide which pieces I wanted to pick up. I'd been unwell and she knew that time spent quietly in wild places was the best way for me to heal. When we arrived at the Lakes, she handed me a guidebook written by Alfred Wainwright. She pointed to a sentence and asked me to read it aloud. It said: "You were made to soar, to crash to earth, then to rise and soar again". How very apt, and how perfect a location for me to recover. The Lake District proved, and still proves, that it is the best place for me to unwind and find myself. It's also one of my favourite places to write.

Writing in the Lake District provides a taste of how life could be if we walked free from the rigours of modern living. With no thoughts of busy jobs, motorways, shopping malls, processed meals, UHT milk and drive-through restaurants, we can settle into a healthier 'pace and place' that restores our inner peace and amplifies our muse's voice. It's just a shame that the pressure of bills and mortgage repayments prevents us from escaping permanently. For most of the time we ring-fence this way of living, reserving it for holiday time and, if we're lucky, weekends where we're free to do pretty much nothing. Of course, it's easy for me to talk like this while I'm on holiday. I've already unwound and am sensing the romance left by people such as Wordsworth, Ruskin, Ransome, Wainwright, and Dalton.

"Dalton?" I hear you ask. Of all these great men, Millican Dalton is most likely to have understood my desired lifestyle. He's was an early advocate for simple and sustainable living, choosing to leave the 'rat race' and begin a new life in the Lakes. Born in 1867, he worked as an insurance clerk in London before turning his back on conventional life at the age of thirty. He made a new living offering 'hair breadth escapes' in The Lake District, where he called himself the 'Professor of Adventure'. He lived in a cave under Castle Crag (in the North-western Fells), slept on a bed of bracken, made his own clothes, grew potatoes, foraged hazelnuts, cooked on an open fire and baked his own bread. He inscribed the entrance to his cave with the message: "Don't waste words, jump to conclusions". It was a fitting motto for a man who washed infrequently, although I prefer his comment made during an interview with the *Daily Mail* in January 1941: "You can't feel lonely with nature as your companion".

Dalton spent forty-nine years living in the wild under canvas, in a cave, or in a makeshift wooden hut. He commented in 1913 that "Camping provides the completest possible change from ordinary town existence and, being the healthiest kind of life as well as the jolliest and most unconventional, is the best antidote to the rush and stress of city work". Ultimately, Dalton demonstrated that we don't have to accept the life we're dealt. We can stay true to our beliefs and exist on our terms. So, as a writer, what are your terms of engagement? How do you measure your success? How do you track how far you've travelled?

Millican Dalton is the inspiration behind my interpretation of the perfect writer's lifestyle. Although we might not be able to abandon modern comforts and live in a cave, we can live by his morals, sleep under canvas once in a while and seek out the freedom to be found in nature. We should think of him when we get dressed for work, especially if we're required to wear black socks that tell us we're stepping into the abyss. 'Dalton' days are different. They're when we can snuggle down with a good book and a warm drink, roll our comfy socks over our feet and be 'properly cosy'. And yet Dalton did not wear socks. He'd already gone one 'step' further. We can travel there too, in our mind's eye, to find our quiet place that encourages us to read and write. Times like these – where we completely escape – are so important. They remind us of who we are, what we feel, and how we choose to see the world. They're havens for our soul. But sometimes we need a little spiritual intervention to help connect us to our higher purpose.

October

XVI

WRITING IN CHURCH

Mrs H and I are still on holiday, spending our time writing, reading, and enjoying the blissful silence of living. There's no television, no radio, no telephone, and no alarm clock. We're making time for each other and the things we love most. If we fancy writing or reading all night, and sleeping all day, then we do. We're keeping to our own hours, waking to the thought of "Hmm, what's for dinner?" and going to bed with a belly full of breakfast. We've not strayed far from the cottage, as we've craved seclusion, though we have enjoyed some evening walks. We've locked ourselves away and relaxed to the point of overachievement, where priorities have been our own. This is a *proper* holiday.

A holiday like this requires a certain mindset. Being so isolated and taking things so slowly (and yet achieving so much) requires an adjustment in both gear and focus. We have to remove our Rocket Man goggles and let go of the missile of modern living. But letting go of a rocket can be risky, especially when it's travelling at supersonic speed. We release our grip, fall, land and tumble, protecting ourselves until we come to rest in a flattened heap upon the ground. Bruised and exhausted, we wonder what just happened and why we've lost the first four days of our holiday.

It's best if the free-fall from work occurs before you pack your suitcase. This isn't easy, especially if you work for the Company Goat who expects you to cram two weeks' work into one before you leave. ("Relax? On work time? Get a Life!") But a holiday should be exactly that: a holiday. Not sick leave, or working time. Don't take your work phone or laptop with you; ensure your 'out of office' and answerphone messages make it clear that you won't be contactable during your vacation.

Sadly I was unable to unwind before my holiday, as too many people wanted a piece of me. So I've made time to adjust now that I'm here. I've walked alone to a quiet place, to practice what I preach. As I Stop – Unplug – Escape – Enjoy, I'll be seeking out the 'peace' of me in a chapel that overlooks the fells.

I'm writing this chapter in surroundings that are cool yet warming, musky yet fresh, dull yet enlightening. I am in a world of outer stillness and inner energy, which makes me want to look up, to see what's below. I am circling, looking for something within my reach but beyond my grasp. A place for many, built for one. I am humbled into pride, inspired into being. In the company of greatness, I pray and write.

The chapel is quiet but not silent. The chatter of a thousand work colleagues has faded, replaced by the hushed voice of a man in dark attire who stands in a pulpit high above me. The vicar of this church doesn't know me, but he's most welcoming. I'm sitting discreetly upon a pew while he's practising his sermon. He's reciting verse from the bible and commenting upon it. His sermon is, so he is saying, based upon Mark 10:46-52. 'Blind Bartimaeus receives his sight.' From what I can gather, it's the story of a blind beggar who, when Jesus passes by, calls to him for help. Jesus hears, they meet, and the man asks if he can be healed. Jesus replies by saying that the man's faith has healed him. The man receives his sight and they go on their way together.

It seems that the vicar's message and my beliefs are the same. If we have faith, then we have direction. If we don't then we are just blind followers, not knowing why we are on the path. And it seems that, like with Bartimaeus, the act of speaking up increases our ability to see. – so long as we trust our voice and believe in our message.

I believe. Because I have faith. When I write, I'm speaking out for what I believe in. For that, I'm grateful.

Faith, in whatever it may be (most especially ourselves and our abilities), keeps us honest and true. It's easier to hear our calling and strive for a meaningful life when we believe in something: a spirit in things or a higher purpose. It's where we writers find our voice and contribute to the True Beauty that defines life's finest creations. But to get there we have to reach deep within, to confront our fears and please our soul. And as I'm in church, I'll share some soulful guidance with you. It's from Mother Teresa, who said: "If you are honest and frank, people may cheat you. Be honest and frank anyway. What you spend years building, someone could destroy overnight. Build anyway. If you find serenity and happiness, they may be jealous. Be happy anyway.

…You see, in the final analysis, it is between you and God. It was never between you and them anyway". How does this sound? Do the words resonate within you? Have you ever shied away from sharing or publishing your work? Do you fear criticism or success? Have you ever lacked faith in your writing ability? Are you too worried about others to properly invest in yourself? If, like me, you share your work with a degree of modesty and shyness, you'll know that the term 'self-confidence' is made up of two conflicting words: confidence isn't easily found in the self. It's one's perception of 'self' that's to blame.

Have you ever described yourself as a 'would-be' writer or 'aspiring' author? There's no would be or aspiring about it. You become a writer every time you pick up a pen. You're an author as soon as your book is published. Your identity is forged by whatever associations and actions define you. However, there's nothing worse to a writer than letting your talents go to waste and saying that you 'used to be' a writer. Keep writing. Every day. Share your message in every possible way. Speak out. Be heard. Be loved. Be the stone that ripples the pond of others' imagination. There are people out there who need you. Be there for them. Share your work.

It's too easy to talk ourselves into a state of inferiority and inertia. Shyness and insecurity breed the words "I can't", which leads to paralysis that can entomb the most promising talent. As the poet Sylvia Plath said, "The worst enemy to creativity is self doubt". She should know. She was found dead with her head in a gas oven at the age of thirty. Her sacrifice proved that we writers must always strive to believe in our ability.

Many writers, myself included, suffer from self-crippling neuroses about their ability. They range from obsessive perfectionism that prevents them from ever being content with anything, to self-doubt that drives fear of sharing their work with anyone. And then there are the self-saboteurs who subconsciously ruin their chances of success – because they secretly fear success more than failure. I've experienced all of these, learning that the greatest rewards are achieved by battling through one's greatest fears. If it scares the hell out of you, then it's worth doing. And doing well.

Whilst modesty and a degree of nervous energy is good, communication is as much about being heard as it is about speaking up. Which is why we writers have to cultivate our confidence to share and promote our work. So, calm your nerves. If your message is strong, it will get through. Writing is easier than speaking – because we have the option to edit our words before sharing them. But alas, editing one's writing can be as easy as lighting a match while riding a bicycle. If you can, get someone else to do it for you.

Committing one's thoughts and feelings to words is like putting one's soul on a plate and hoping the diners will like what they eat. But not everyone's tastes are the same. It's a case of, 'some will like the dish and ask for more; others will heave and spew on the floor'. And that's to be expected. Better to be remarkable – for good or bad – than to be ignored.

'Wearing one's heart on one's sleeve' and 'sticking one's head above the parapet' are clichés that warn a writer about the risks of writing about his or her beliefs. But, as Mother Teresa might say, we "do it anyway". And for good reason: we have something to say.

For each person who writes openly and honestly, or dares to be different, there are a dozen or more conformists who will ridicule the writer, hoping to push him or her into a submissive and silent state. They choose to belittle the individual for being, 'individual'. *"For showing flair, talent and confidence – that we secretly lack – is punishable by public mockery. SO BE THE SENTENCE."* My artist friend Bert describes such critics as "Short-sighted pigmies, poking their stubby little fingers into things they don't understand". He's not joking. There's a fine line between fair criticism and jealous assault. Subjected writers can lose courage to share their magic with the world. Their creative spark fades and – like nodding dogs on the parcel shelf of a Ford Fiesta – they're carried through life in perpetual acceptance of everything around them. But writers have inner strength. It drives them to keep writing, regardless of whatever is thrown in their path. So I say this: "See your destiny and pursue it. Break through your fears. Move forward with every word written upon the page. Each one lifts you higher, helping you to walk free from the long shadows cast by small people". Seek only feedback from those whom you trust, and ignore the rest. As Andy Warhol said: "Don't read your reviews, weigh them".

It seems that those who ridicule people for being creative, artistic, poetic, romantic, or a bit daft, are really just fearful of their own lack of creativity.

Modern society – the same one that fears stepping outdoors in case it loses its Wi-Fi or mobile phone signal – favours logical, rational thought. And here is the irony: that a society which places great emphasis on mathematical and scientific knowledge, which praises analytical thinking and level-headed behaviour and sees qualifications or professions in the arts as being somehow inferior, requires creative people to entertain it.

I have a mantra that says: "Exams test your memory, life tests your learning; others will test your patience". What does it matter if we creative folk look or behave differently, or if our tastes are different to others? Why should we change that which makes us unique? There's no need for revisions or indecisions. We should be and act how we want. If how we live pleases us, and doesn't cause any harm, then we alone judge whether we have succeeded or failed. We are all Clapping Monkeys; but while some of us smile, others look around to see if anyone has noticed.

Of course, it's better to surround yourself with people who support and encourage you. It was Mrs H and my close friends Isaac and Prof who placed a barrel of petrol onto my creative fire. Tired of giving me 'gentle persuasion' to share my writing, they gave me an ultimatum: "Publish a book before you're too old to read it without glasses". So I set to work, writing with renewed focus. The result was *A Meaningful Life*, the first book in the Fennel's Journal series. It's published now, testament to a promise I made to pursue my dreams no matter what the cost. The fear of failing to please them, or failing to pursue my dreams, became more motivating than the fear of ridicule for trying. But successes and failures, like the tastes of our audience, are very personal. A book is successful if it enhances just one person's life, even if that life is your own. You don't need your book to make it onto a bestseller list. Those lists bolster the publisher's ego more than the author's. Remember that communication is only ever, and can only ever be, one-to-one. Speak to one person, and let them hear you. Change them for the better.

Let your writing speak for you. It's where your words land, and how they're collected and interpreted, that counts. I could be writing this with a cushion on my head and a pink parrot on my left shoulder. I could be scrawling in chalk onto a dirty pavement, or writing words one at a time onto pieces of paper and floating them down a river. It doesn't matter. Whichever way I present these words, you will be the one making sense of them. In this respect, you've got the best job. The best job of all: because these words will register differently with you than with anyone else. That's why it's important for us writers to speak openly and honestly. The odd word might go by unnoticed, and what your reader's left with might be a bit soggy around the edges, but it's us on the page.

Here I am: Fennel, the one who thought he'd never have the confidence to speak up; who hid away from trouble, never believing that anyone would want to listen to his words or see things as he does. I'm the one who proved them wrong, by pursuing my dreams and crushing my fears. This book is testament to everything we writer's desire: to be bound to our reader in silence between the covers of a book, speaking loudly for them to hear.

Nature or nurture? A talent needs both. But it requires the individual to know the basis and beauty of his or her nature, and to understand that neglecting their skill is to go against the very core of their being. It is a crime against their maker. Writing in church helps us to connect with our spirit and understand our purpose. It helps us to realise that not using a talent to the best of our ability is to stifle the thing that makes us most special. It's like plucking the wings off a butterfly.

If you find comfort in writing, people may mock your pen and spit in your ink. Write anyway.

Stop – Unplug – Escape – Enjoy

How much do you believe in your ability? Are you giving everything you can to your talents and passions?

November

XVII

THE CREATIVE FIRE

"Remember, remember, the 5th of November." Why? Because it's one of the best nights of the year, that's why. A proper burn-up in the garden, with sparklers, fireworks and a tray full of jacket potatoes. It's my sort of evening. Oh yes, and there's something about a 'guy' trying to blow up the House of Lords. But that's an afterthought when presented with a *Sonic Skythunder* rocket that requires two people to carry it, has to be launched from a concrete bunker, and would most likely trigger World War III.

I jest, of course.

Bonfire Night is a historic occasion that acknowledges the greatest conspirator in British history. Even if people forget the event of 1605, they shouldn't forget four hundred years of tradition that celebrates King James surviving the assassination attempt. But to us writers, bonfires make us think about creativity and passion. If we're 'fired up' and 'burning brightly', we're likely to be producing our best work.

We writers constantly seek inspiration to keep our creative fires burning. Always looking for our next idea, news story, or angle; we'll be reading every available situation, exploring every opportunity, and every source of information. We'll always be looking, listening, feeling and thinking. But be cautious of the point when all this information becomes a distraction.

Attentiveness is fine when one's radar is aimed at specific things, but it's a curse when we're casting our gaze (or creative net) too wide. Just think of all the chatter out there that can eat up our valuable writing time, diluting our energy and distracting us from the wonderful words that wrestle to be free.

Whilst bonfire night is a celebratory time to be shared with others, please strive to ensure that your creative fire avoids the distractions of metaphorical fireworks that overwhelm your senses. Stay focused on the fire, and fan the flames. This is why I'm writing this chapter at 10pm while gazing at the embers of our annual bonfire. I'm transfixed by the swirling yellows, reds, whites, blues and greens of flames rising from the glowing timber. They're illuminating my writing pad with colours that dance with kaleidoscopic merriment.

This year's fire holds extra significance for me. It was lit atop a pile of notebooks I'd written last year and had since typed up into neat. There must have been three hundred-or-so of them, each crammed with my daily jottings and ideas. I doubt if I'll ever write so much in a year again, as I'm unlikely to spend another year living alone beside a lake, so setting light to them was ceremonial – like a cremation rather than a bonfire. All those thoughts captured on the page, burning and rising skywards. A million words or more, all drifting back into the ether from where they came.

Not all the books, however, were burned. One caught my attention as I added it to the pile. It lacked the usual splodges of mud and smudges of ink of the ones written by the lake, and was too small to have been used in my study. I picked it up and realised that it was one that had been handed out at a writing conference earlier this year. In it were the notes I'd made while listening to the keynote speech. The notes were short but compelling. They read:

"Rules for creativity and innovation:

1) Know who you are and where you come from. *Your brand is important. Be clear of your purpose and message.*
2) Don't do anything unless you're interested in it. *Be interested.*
3) Stop doing things when you've stopped learning. *Never be bored.*
4) It's difficult to learn unless you make new relationships. *Proactively network with influential people, sustain these relationships. Be there for them.*
5) It helps to be slightly possessed and eccentric. *Be compelled by white-hot passion and fury to succeed. Strive to be the most intense version of your true self.*
6) Don't look or wait too long before you leap. *Leap, even if you're not completely ready.*
7) Opportunity builds capability. *Crisis helps you improvise and curiosity compels you to do things that interest you.*

8) Don't get trapped at your desk. *Ideas come from a change of scenery once your mind has cleared.*

9) Have a real sense of mission. *If it drives you, you don't need to drive it.*

10) Borrow ideas and combine them into a new context; say and hear things you didn't expect; challenge conventional wisdom. *Creating stories will draw people and resources to them."*

The notes read like a ten-step process of how to fan one's creative fire. I decided to keep the notebook as a memento of bonfire night, and have included the steps here to remind us to maintain our 'real sense of mission'.

Fire gives warmth and illuminates. Smoke clouds but adds flavour. Flames mesmerise with beauty and terror. An elemental force, compelling us towards the flame. But a fire without a heart will soon die. Always feed the fire, keeping the timbers close to its heart. Fan the flames, hear it roar. Remember, remember, you're a writer. Remember?

December

XVIII

THE LOST STORY OF A LOST PEN

Mrs H and I will soon be moving house. Good thing, too, as I'm desperately in need of more space. With a thousand-or-so books amassed over the past twenty-five years, I need twice as many bookshelves again if I am to continue reading and collecting at the same rate for the rest of my life. I'm excited by the prospect of being able to buy more books. But Mrs H sees the house move as an opportunity for us to have a clear-out.

John Ruskin said, "every increased possession loads us with a new weariness". Unfortunately for Mrs H, the quote doesn't apply to me. I am a hoarder of anything and everything. Things that have meaning to me would be worthless to anyone else. My study contains pens that don't work, hats that don't fit, teacups with broken handles, mould-crusted bottles, bits of rubble, bottles of lake water and a teapot named Ethelred the Unsteady that I bought in a factory seconds shop. Disturbing this clutter would be like conducting an archaeological dig at a rubbish dump. Items would need to be carefully removed, dated and placed into cardboard boxes lined with cotton wool. Which is why I'm under pressure. Mrs H instructed me to 'do my best' and then handed me an entire roll of dustbin bags.

I was bold at first, throwing away the first things that came to hand (three spent matchsticks and a box of rusty paperclips). But hoarder's palpitations have caused me to stop. It was too much, too soon. I needed to be sure I was doing the right thing. I needed a robust selection process. Yes, that was it. I needed to be methodical. A black and white 'in or out' criteria, such as: if it wasn't mine, it could go.

I started with the boxes under my desk. I opened one of them. Just one. It's in front of me now, sitting on my desk, quaking in fear. The box has the words 'college stuff, 1996' written on it. It has lived with me unopened in six different houses. But now that I've broken the seal of dried parcel tape and dust, I can see that it contains sketchbooks, paintbrushes, pencils, graphite sticks, dip pens, bottles of ink, tubes of paint, rolls of drafting tape, exercise books, study guides and, what's this? My old fountain pen. Ooh. *My old fountain pen.*

The pen was once my favourite. I had it as a teenager, it saw me through college and university. It was destined for great things. I was to use it to write my books and articles, maybe even for book signings. Alas, it's also the one I chucked in a box and forgot about for 12 years. A sad fate for such a lovely pen. It's a gold-trimmed Waterman that once had a translucent emerald finish. But the paint has perished and lies as flakes of green at the bottom of the box. What's left of the pen is actually quite nice: a polished chrome barrel and cap, and a gold nib that glows in the candlelight of my study. The ink within it has dried, and the ink filler looks clogged, so I'm going soak the pen in warm water. It will be a baptism of sorts, a rebirth for a new future that will connect me with my past. A continuity of words and love of writing, held within this pen. I shall name it *Perpetuitas*.

Bear with me while I nip to the kitchen, get a bowl of water, and put the pen in to soak.

Okay, I'm back. The pen's soaking and blue ink is seeping into the water. It'll be running clear in half an hour. Just long enough to tell you about the pen and its history.

The pen was present, given to me for my sixteenth birthday by my parents. It was part of a gift that also included an *Oxford English Dictionary* and *Roget's Thesaurus*. They were inscribed 'For your next book'. I was, at the time, obsessed with reading and writing everything I could, at every opportunity (no change there, then). Romantic poetry was my teenage religion; works by Wordsworth, Keats, Shelley, Coleridge, and Byron were filling my bookshelves. I emulated their style, writing scores of poems that helped me to comprehend my place within the world.

The fountain pen wrote thousands of words during its first six years. It penned everything from college essays to my first curriculum vitae. Then 1996 arrived. It was the fateful year when I left university and stashed the pen in the box of college bits. Like so many things in my study, the college box became hidden amongst the clutter of an overly sentimental person. The pen, and the story that went with it, got lost. But now they are found. Entwined once more, to continue the story.

Some Golden Rules for writing, written

with the rejuvenated pen, will be its first task. But before then, a reflection: the pen that was once a gift has come to represent all that I hope to achieve. It's a reminder of the writer I was, the one I am, and the author I will become.

Fine Things such as my lost pen remind me of who I am. They're emblems of identity that belong in my study, as it's the place where I'm most at home. And yet they're "yet another thing to clutter up the house", as Mrs H might argue. Good thing, too, as they've distracted me from the job at hand. I'm supposed to be emptying my creative zone.

Work to do, or not to do, I shall go downstairs and tell Mrs H that the purge is taking longer than expected. Of course, you and I know that it will take much longer than she thinks. I have no intention of decluttering my study. It's perfect just the way it is. And it's *all* coming with me.

I am Fennel the writer. This is my book. The one I've written for you. Let it always remain in your study, reminding you to pursue your dreams. Never let go of that which inspires you.

Bonus Chapter 2017

XIX

THE GOLDEN RULES OF WRITING

Ernest Hemmingway wrote: "I learned never to empty the well of my writing, but always to stop when there was still something there in the deep part of the well, and let it refill at night from the springs that feed it". Wise words from one of the greatest modern-day writers, and sage advice to someone challenged with emptying his study, but hauntingly sad given the periods in his later life where – paralysed by depression and paranoia – he was unable to write.

I've found there to be no such thing as writer's block. As Terry Pratchett wrote, "there's always an angle, and always a way". Writing, however, is closely linked to sensitivity and perception. It encourages happiness, contemplation and creation. There's much to be found in the quiet loneliness of silent observation. It's where genius sparks like midnight lightning on a moonless night. But it's also where dark clouds consume us when our muse goes quiet.

Managing one's writing output is easier when one's emotions are in check. Also when one learns from experience and follows a process. Which is why I'm going to share some tips with you. I call them my Golden Rules of Writing.

Fennel's Golden Rules of Writing

1. Know and stay true to your brand. Every word you write must support your brand promise and values.

2. Know your voice. Dare to be different. How does your message, or how you say it, make you unique? What can you write about, in a way that no one else can?

3. Be clear about your message and mission. Decide what you want to say, and the reaction (or action) you seek from your reader, and then make your point quickly – ideally in the first paragraph. Or, more interestingly, by describing something in an abstract way that forces your reader to take notice and see things as you do.

4. Be clear about your message and mission. Sounds familiar? It's so important, I've listed it twice. It means writing with purpose. Know exactly what you want your reader to know, understand, do, or feel as a result of reading your writing. Begin with this end in mind. Have a macro message (that readers will know you for) and a micro message that will be the focus of your book, chapter, or article.

5. Have an angle. Decide the perspective you wish to apply to a subject, then use the story to 'show not tell' your observations to your reader. The goal is to make the reader observe something they perhaps hadn't thought of before (hence why I developed my rule of 'Inspire, Inform, Entertain' – selecting one or more as the goal for each chapter or article I write).

6. Keep things simple. Have just one message, angle or argument in your writing. Reinforce it (ideally three times), either from different perspectives or by giving supporting examples. The Rule of Three is invaluable.

7. *Structure your writing.* Each book, chapter and article should have a beginning, middle and end. The beginning sets the scene, providing the background and context of what you will write next. The middle is the story that supports your message, and the end is either the conclusion (learning), page turner (cliff hanger), or call to action. Again, The Rule of Three.

8. *Don't circle.* Keep the tense and timeline consistent. If you're telling a story, the reader expects you to guide them through a logical timeline, so don't 'circle' from past, present, and future events or tense.

9. *Write passionately.* Whilst you might temper your emotion, never temper your passion. Always, always, write passionately. People are unlikely to remember your exact words, but they'll remember the story and how you made them feel. So make them feel your passion. Always consider and shape the emotional reaction you want your reader to have at various points during the story, and especially how you want them to feel at the end.

10. *Inspire your reader.* There's a marketing rule that says 'people react to wants, not needs'. For example, if you're a food writer, you could write about the nutritional value of the muscles on a pig's back. But you'd inspire your reader more if you wrote about how amazing it is to wake to the smell and sound of bacon frying in a pan. Make them want to take action.

11. *Use Plain English.* You'll lose your reader if he or she has to keep reaching for a dictionary. As you gain

experience and confidence, use the thesaurus less and less. Always speak with language appropriate to your audience. Less is usually more, so use words economically, removing superfluous text and unnecessary adjectives. The first word you think of is usually best, so don't feel compelled to be 'clever' with your word choices.

12. Speak with a conversational tone. It makes your writing more accessible. Use 'it's' not 'it is' unless you're stressing a point or writing for formal or academic publications. Usually, though, people like to hear your voice when reading your words, so write as you would speak. Use simple word choices and make only one point per sentence. If you get stuck, use a Dictaphone and then transcribe your words to observe your tone and style. I bet you use shorter sentences and paragraphs than you realised. This is good.

13. Writing is entertainment. People choose to invest their time and money in reading, so make it worthwhile. Give them something they value, and sometimes things they didn't expect but then come to love. Your writing has to compete for their attention, not just with other authors but also with television programmes, films, computer games, and a whole host of recreations.

14. Make your writing personal. Always write as if you're talking to one person, not a group. Remember: you're one person, your reader is one person. Always try to picture the person you're writing to. If it helps, have a photo of them on your desk and start your article or chapter with 'Dear ...' (then remove the 'Dear' bit during editing). Also remember that 'you' and 'we' are power words that get the reader on your side.

15. For your reader, everything is now. You might have written the material many years before, but it's present in the reader's world today. You may have moved on in your interests, tastes or research, but as far as your reader is concerned, your words are a snapshot of your world right now. So provide continuity or a gradual evolution of the messages and values communicated in your writing. Take the reader on your journey, but at their pace.

16. Make your reader smile. Conflict presents an opportunity for comedy. The classic sitcom is based on this principle. It entertains your reader and makes your story more memorable. Remember Ted the Postman's replacement, or the man on the train doing the crossword? What memorable ways to emphasise the allure and power of words.

17. Make it real. If you're introducing characters, ensure they support your overall story. There are three types of character: Protagonist, Victim, and Rescuer. Each character relates to the other. In Fennel's Journal, protagonists include harsh employers, urban places, blind acceptance of modern technology, and sedentary indoor lifestyles. They make me the victim. Rescuers are Mrs H, nature, writing, traditionalism, and outdoor adventure. They free me from the victimisation caused by the protagonists. See how it works?

18. Enable your reader to escape. Atmosphere and emotion bring writing to life. Take the reader with you on your adventures as you explore places and subjects. Evoke the senses. Build images in the reader's mind. Use verbs relating to hearing, seeing, feeling, tasting and smelling. If we can picture it, it's more likely to seem real and the writer-reader bond will develop.

19. Write for yourself... Unless you're writing marketing copy or ghost-writing something for someone else, write firstly about things that inspire you. Writing for a particular audience's needs can be draining. Worse, it can dilute your uniqueness as you kowtow to what's safe and expected. Be true to your unique voice and the worldview for which you're known. Maintain the angle in your writing. Hold true to it, as your readers want your view, not someone else's.

20. ...but know your audience. Present your passions in a way that resonates with your reader's worldview. Spend at least 25% of your time researching them. Read about them. Read what they read. Know what excites them. Know their values. Spend time with them (face-to-face or virtually, in forums and on social media). Know what issues affect them. Follow the mantra of: "What do they value most? How can I deliver it better than other authors? And if I write it, and they read it, will we both have fun?"

21. Spend less time writing. Follow the 40-20-40 rule: 40% of your time planning what you'll write, 20% writing the first draft, 40% proofreading and editing.

22. Read more than you write. Read all forms of writing, not just your genre. If you get to 'feel' the way other writers describe things and structure their messages, you'll be able to replicate and blend their styles to create the effect you want. Learn the meter, pace and tone used to captivate the reader. Study the writing of the most successful authors in the business: Agatha

Christie for whodunnits; Barbara Cartland or Danielle Steel for romance; Harold Robbins for suspense; Tom Clancey, Dan Brown or John Grisham for page-turning thrillers; Stephen King for horror; JK Rowling or JRR Tolkien for fantasy; Roald Dahl for children's fiction; Douglas Adams or Terry Pratchett for fantasy humour; PG Wodehouse for comedy; Arthur C Clarke or HG Wells for science fiction; and so on.

23. Always have a notepad and pen to hand. I have notebooks all over the house, and in every rucksack and coat. You're most likely to be creative when your mind is occupied with mundane tasks, or is sleepy. (Research 'left-brain and right-brain theory'.) So, as a minimum, a notebook in the car or on the bedside table is a must. The rule? Write things down before you forget them.

24. Build a support network. Follow the Stephen King rule of "Plan with the door open, write with the door shut, and edit with the door open". It implies that although writing is a solitary vocation, always seek the help, inspiration and encouragement of others at the appropriate times. This is at the beginning and end of the process, not the middle. (When writing you need as few distractions as possible).

25. Follow a process. Here's the one I use:

a) Brainstorm the subject. Create a mind map that explores subjects, groups ideas and angles, and has bold or dotted lines that link things in obvious or obscure ways. Is the direction of travel for your writing obvious?

b) Storyboard. Turn your mind map into a storyboard by structuring it as bullet points in the order in which you'll write (e.g. one bullet point per paragraph or chapter, with sub-bullets that explore and debate the point in more detail, remembering The Rule of Three).

c) *Write the first draft.* It's important at this stage to just write and not edit – challenging your fingers to keep up with your thoughts. Don't worry too much about typos or correcting things as you go – you can do this later. Just get your thoughts down. If you write with a pen, do it with your eyes closed to prevent the temptation of reading or editing as you go.

d) *Edit and polish up the draft.* Correct the typos and grammar, edit out any superfluous text, and check that your intended message is clear. Ensure an economical use of words (balanced, of course, with a reader-friendly conversational writing style) and ensure you're not over your intended or commissioned word count. Check for the correct use of words, the intended pace and flow (single word sentences are a great way of making an impact. Truth.) Follow the rule: 'if in doubt, cut it out'.

e) *Read it aloud.* Give it a read through, reading aloud to aid punctuation and to ensure a natural conversational voice. Do a second edit where necessary.

f) *Put aside the draft.* Give it time to 'breathe'. It's important to rest your work before you edit it again. As a minimum leave it for a few hours, but ideally for a few weeks. This allows you to view it again with fresh eyes – spotting all the errors that you were blind to before.

g) *Do a proofread.* Perhaps the biggest risk to a writer is proofreading your own work. If you don't know a rule of grammar, it's unlikely that you'll have learnt it by the time you get to the editing stage. Ideally get someone else to do the proofreading – and potentially a third person to critique it. But if you don't have someone suitably skilled to do this, then print out your work (this is important, as we read differently on paper to on a screen) and read it aloud *slowly*. If it doesn't sound right, it probably isn't.

h) *Do a super critical – and very slow – final read through*. Again, use a printed copy. Use a pencil or pen to track each word, one at a time, checking for typos and misspellings. Anticipate your readers' reactions and viewpoints, ensure all statements will stand up to scrutiny, and check that your intended message is clear.

i) When you're absolutely happy, *submit for publication*.

There you have it: 25 points to help your writing. What binds these points together? Clarity of message and brutal editing. As Ernest Hemingway said, "The most essential gift for a good writer is a built-in, shockproof, shit detector. This is the writer's radar and all great writers have had it". If you are to become expert at one thing, it's in spotting poor writing and correcting it. (Something that challenges us all.) But don't beat yourself up if you miss something. When you receive your author's proof, allow yourself leniency for errors that have somehow remained, or things you'd like to change. There will inevitably be some. I use a credit system, allocating twenty credits for a book and one for an article.

A credit is used each time I spot an error or desired chang. (See, I just lost one then.) If I have any credits remaining at the end of the final read-through, then I use them to fund my writer's reward. And it's worthwhile, as each of my credits is worth a glass of wine. Like it? What will be your reward?

These are my Golden Rules of Writing. Practise them in the writing you do every day. Seek the story and the angle. Live to write, and write to live. As Douglas Pagels said, "Each new day is a blank page in the diary of your life. The secret of success is in turning that diary into the best story you possibly can."

XX

LOOK BACK,
BUT NEVER LOOK DOWN

It was my father who gave me the stern but encouraging advice to "Look back, but don't look down". A qualified Mountain Leader, Dad was used to assessing imminent risks and ensuring the safety of his party. His instruction to me was in response to my sudden panic while climbing a rock face in Snowdonia. I was one of seven boys on a school adventure trip. All my friends had completed the climb and were peering over the ledge above me. But I was stuck, frozen to the cliff, terrified of falling to my death or, worse, being humiliated by my friends if I failed. I barely had a foothold and most of my weight was held on my fingertips. My arms were shaking. Time was moving too slowly. I attempted to prise a finger from the rock. But it was no good. I was paralysed by fear.

"Dad, I can't."

"Keep going!" cried the spectators above.

I closed my eyes and tried to pull myself up. But I felt my grip weaken and slip. I opened my eyes and saw the sky swirling as I fell from the rock. A moment of weightlessness and then – firm hands around my waist.

"Look back." repeated my father. I turned my head

to see him with raised arms, holding me firmly at head height. I was barely five feet off the ground.

Self-doubt is the biggest handicap for anyone wishing to achieve anything. It can be mentally and physically debilitating. I'd proven this by failing to climb a rock face within seconds of starting, when my friends had succeeded with relative ease. I might have been smaller and weaker than them, but I lacked the will to succeed and the want to endure. It was this that caused me to fail. I'd conceded before I began.

I can't. These are words that should never be on the lips of anyone wishing to pursue their dreams. Especially if that dream is to be a writer. There's always a way. Education, experience, opportunity and – most importantly – self-belief. But when things do go your way, beware your ego. You're a writer with a job to do. Leave your peacock on the lawn.

So, a Rule of Three to end with:

1. *Practice your craft.* Feel, in every second of every minute spent writing, a compulsion that drives you to become that which you dream of being.

2. *Finish your book.* You're writing so that others can read. It's about making it to the summit, standing atop a mountain of hopes and dreams, with book in hand shouting: "I did this!"

3. *Appreciate your achievements.* Drink your wine or enjoy whatever reward you choose. But whilst reflection is good, don't let it distract you from your future dreams and next project. Marvel at how far you've come, but don't revisit old ground.

Look back, but never look down.

ABOUT THE AUTHOR

FENNEL HUDSON

"Author, artist, naturalist and countryman. His is a lifestyle to inspire the most bricked-up townie."

Fennel Hudson is an author, blogger, letter writer, magazine contributor and public speaker. He's published fourteen books in the *Fennel's Journal* series, writes the weekly *Fennel on Friday* blog and hosts *The Contented Countryman* podcast. By day he's an award-winning copywriter and authority in the art of writing sales proposals. With more than thirty million of his words in print, you'd think he'd be tiring of the craft. But his passion remains, especially for writing letters with a vintage fountain pen onto quality paper.

For more information please visit:
www.fennelspriory.com

THE FENNEL'S JOURNAL SERIES

THE FIRST-EVER REVIEWS OF FENNEL'S JOURNAL:

"Fennel's Journal began as a series of illustrated letters to friends. As these evolved they became less a diary, more a manifesto, and the Journal is now exactly that – a way of living, rurally and simply: very real for all those who recognise the importance of tradition and joy."

Caught by the River

"I can see where it might lead. What he has would make amazing TV. It's the Good Life, but in a realistic way. It's Jack Hargreaves. It's Countryfile. It's quality Sunday newspaper stuff. It's 1948, all over again. In trying to escape the present he's inevitably created a brand. A potentially very powerful brand."

Bob Roberts Online

"Fennel's Journal is a masterpiece about rural living. It is a route-map to the life we all seek."

The Traditional Fisherman's Forum

From A Meaningful Life:

"Life is the most beautiful and rewarding gift. We just need to take time out to allow us to reflect, change perspective, and see things in their best light. Sometimes we just have to stop and feel the pulse of the Earth, the rhythm of the seasons and the internal voice that was once our childhood friend. As the natural world grows smaller, so too does its intensity and the size of the window through which it may be viewed."

NO.1

A MEANINGFUL LIFE

A Meaningful Life is the first and perhaps most important Journal. It documents the origins of Fennel's Priory and why Fennel decided to live by a new set of ideals. With themes ranging from escapism, adventure, work-life balance, identity and purpose, through to traditionalism and country living, it sets the scene for future editions – building messages that are central to Fennel's Priory. Ultimately it conveys the importance of a relaxed, balanced, and meaningful life.

READER TESTIMONIALS

"I loved reading this Journal. It's inspiring and has the beginnings of something very special."

"Fennel's chosen trajectory is firmly in the slow lane. He's a countryman, with courage to stand behind his traditional values."

"Witty and emotive, Fennel's writing conveys passion for a slower-paced and quieter life."

From A Waterside Year:

"Water is intrinsically linked to the mystery and excitement of discovering new worlds. Of dreams. And hopes. And thoughts of what 'could be'. Dreams free us from normality. ...As the daydreams grew longer, the distinction between what was real and what was imaginary grew less. Soon I existed in a blissful world of my own creation. Reality, as I learned, is only a matter of perception...A life that is real to one is surreal to another."

NO. 2

A WATERSIDE YEAR

In *A Waterside Year*, Fennel takes time out to live beside a lake in rural England. Here he appreciates the healing qualities of water, studies the wildlife around him, lives at the pace of someone outside of normal daily life, and discovers the freedom that's found in isolation. Getting so close to Nature, and spending time in idle fashion, enables him to discover a stronger sense of self. Ultimately he learns that freedom is not a place, but something that exists within us.

READER TESTIMONIALS

"A year in the wild. How we would all love to follow in Fennel's stead and indulge our dreams, to come out the other side a stronger and wiser person."

"A Journal with a message – that we should take time out to think about what's important, and see the beauty of the world."

"A truly blissful read full of inspiration and humour. The story of Fennel sitting in his tent, with the noises outside, had me laughing out loud!"

From A Writer's Year:

"Writing, with a fountain pen and ink from a bottle, is the simplest of things. Yet it can transport us to a different place entirely. Imagination is the real magic that exists in this world. Look inwards, to see outwards. And capture it in writing."

NO. 3

A WRITER'S YEAR

A Writer's Year celebrates the writer's craft. It champions the handwritten letter, discusses vintage pens and writing ink, and celebrates things such as antique typewriters and the quirkiness of the creative mind. It's a blend of observations. It's funny. It's serious. It's real life. But most of all it is written to encourage aspiring authors to find their voice, to put pen to paper, and follow their dreams.

READER TESTIMONIALS

"Worth it for the first chapter alone. It cannot fail to motivate and inspire the would-be author."

"What Fennel has written is not so much a eulogy for the handwritten letter as a call-to-arms for everyone to follow their dreams and make the most of their God-given talents. This is a genuinely inspiring read."

"I loved the part: 'If a pen can communicate our thoughts, dreams and emotions and be the voice of our soul, then ink is the medium that carries the message'. It shows how important and generous writing can be."

From Wild Carp:

"Some will say that searching for your dreams is like looking for unicorns in an emerald forest. They will say that following a golden thread will lead only to a king, dethroned and living in the gutter. This may be so.
But the king was made, not born.
The crown was never his to wear.
...If ever the adventure proves tiring, or you lose sight of your dream, look to the west at sunset. There, on days when the skies are clear, you might see upon the horizon a thin layer of golden mist. When it appears, you will know its purpose: it is
the mist of believing."

NO. 4

WILD CARP

Angling for wild carp is about adventure, history, atmosphere and emotion. *Wild Carp* captures this aplenty, describing Fennel's 20-year quest to find a very special type of fish. But it's also about nature connection and a desire to uncover the seemingly impossible – a place where we can discover and live out our dreams, to completely indulge the mantra of 'Stop – Unplug – Escape – Enjoy'.

READER TESTIMONIALS

"When written well, traditional angling writing by the likes of BB, for example, is the type of literature that I can read again and again. Fennel's writing flows un-hurried without overly romanticising each point and the research is thorough; from the first sentence I was thinking, 'this lad can write!' It's informative and very refreshing."

"Such inspiring writing. His words 'Somewhere in the undergrowth of the impossible' had me staring out from the page in amazement. Fennel's writing is pure poetry."

From Fly Fishing:

"The deeper we travel into the natural world, and the greater the number of technological encumbrances we leave behind, the more likely we are to escape the fast-paced lifestyle and stresses of the 21st Century. For some, angling enables a quest into the unknown, an adventure into the wild. For these fortunate folk, fly-fishing is escapism. Their hours by water serve as contemplation to enrich their souls, directing their quest inwards, towards their longed-for state of completeness."

NO. 5

FLY FISHING

Fly Fishing celebrates the most graceful and artful form of angling, explaining what it means to be an angler – in the spirit of Izaak Walton – and how fly fishers differ from bait fishers. The sporting and aesthetic beauty of fly-fishing is described in Fennel's usual witty and contemplative style. As he says, "Fly fishing is the ultimate form of angling; it gives us a reason to fish simply, travel lightly, and explore wild places that replenish our soul. With a fly rod, we're not casting to a fish; rather to a circle of dreams: ripples that spread into every aspect of our lives".

READER TESTIMONIALS

"Brilliant writing. Fennel made me laugh out loud in bed. My wife was asking questions!"

"A delightful, well-articulated, read. I strongly recommend it, especially to the contemplative, tradition-loving, bamboo fly rod devotees among us."

"A very inspiring and rewarding read. I will try to tie the Sedgetastic fly. It looks tasty!"

From Traditional Angling:

"Physics teaches us that for every action, there is an equal and opposite reaction: a natural balance of energy that sustains the equilibrium of life. In modern angling, these forces are skewed so far in favour of technology that the balance between science and art has been lost. But there is a movement, an undercurrent that defies the flow of progress. There are those who choose not to follow the crowd. They seek not to fish in a predictable, scientific manner. They yearn for the opposite, to buck the trend, *to be different*. They are the Traditional Anglers."

NO. 6

TRADITIONAL ANGLING

Traditional Angling celebrates the Waltonian values of angling: about fishing in a seasonal and uncompetitive way for the pure pleasure of being beside water. It wears its heart on its sleeve and a wildflower in its lapel. It's passionate, provocative and eccentric, written for those who appreciate the aesthetics of angling and uphold its sporting traditions. So, with great enthusiasm, raise your bamboo rod aloft for an adventure that proves there's more to fishing than catching fish.

READER TESTIMONIALS

"A beautifully written, very engaging and hugely enjoyable read. In fact, it's the best thing on fishing I've read in a long time."

"What a Journal! Fennel is clearly the spiritual successor to his mentor – the great Bernard Venables. There's so much wisdom and craftsmanship in his writing. Bernard clearly taught him very well."

From The Quiet Fields:

"The countryside, with its vast horizons, fresh air and ever-changing seasons is, by its very nature, more life-giving and adventurous than any amount of modern indoor living. It inspires a love of natural history – everything from the birds that sing in the trees to the quality and richness of the soil beneath our feet. Most of all, it creates the desire to exist more naturally. And in doing so, we appreciate the balance of life."

NO. 7

THE QUIET FIELDS

The Quiet Fields is rooted in the humus-rich soil of the countryside. It's about remote rural places where Nature exists undisturbed, where we may sit and ponder 'The Wonder of the World'. The Journal tips its hat to these places, and to the nature writing of BB, revealing the 'Lost England' that still exists if you know where and how to look. It is the most sentimental and astutely observed Journal to date, discussing the 'true beauty' of Nature. If you've ever yearned to hear birdsong during a busy day, then this is the book for you.

READER TESTIMONIALS

"Fennel's writing reminds me of the works of Roger Deakin. It inspires me with faith in the quiet life and that although I may be isolated, I am certainly not alone."

"Fennel has captured the essence of the countryside — that is, its almost human character. So brilliantly has he compared and contrasted it with the nature of we humans. It's not so much a 'balanced study', more a 'study of the balance' between Nature and Man."

From Fine Things:

"It seems that, depending upon which side of the thesaurus-writer's gaze we sit, one's uniqueness as a person can be deemed to be either eccentric or distinctive. Both, in my opinion, are good...As we get older, and experience more things, those of us with strength of character and a sense of purpose will grow stronger and fight harder; those who lack identity and direction might end up sitting in a corner somewhere, blindly taking all the knocks that life throws at them. What does this teach us? That character and purpose are directly linked to confidence and conviction. What links them? Courage – to be oneself, no matter what others might say."

NO. 8

FINE THINGS

Fine Things celebrates the special and sentimental items and activities that convey our personality. The writing is fast-paced, quirky and humorous, reflecting the author's enthusiasm and eccentric view of the world. But be warned: if you look inside Fennel's mind, you might see a hula-hooping hamster named Gerald, shaking his maracas, loudly banging a bongo, and getting him into all sorts of trouble. So strap yourself in. This book picks up pace and takes some unexpected turns. From the deeply personal to the outright eccentric, it's for those who seek to be different.

READER TESTIMONIALS

"A very fine thing, indeed. Fennel's best and funniest book to date. He is the only author who can make me laugh out loud and cry in the same sentence. I was constantly in tears, for all the right reasons."

"Deep in places, outright bonkers in others. A demonstration of the fine line between genius and madness."

From A Gardener's Year:

"Roll up your sleeves and imagine your vision of paradise. This, in whatever form it takes, is your garden. Keep hold of the image; know it's every detail and piece together the elements that need creating or nurturing, so that when you get the chance, you can prepare the ground, sow the seeds, and make it real. Ours is a gardener's life, whether we realise it or not."

NO. 9

A GARDENER'S YEAR

A Gardener's Year celebrates the joy of growing things and reflects upon a life working with plants. But it's not a record of horticultural activities through the seasons. It's a metaphor for having a dream and making it come true. For Fennel, who has spent half his life working in gardens, it's about cultivating a cottage garden where he can aspire to a self-sufficient lifestyle. The Journal sees him sow the seeds of this future reality.

READER TESTIMONIALS

"Fennel's writing is uniquely funny. I mean, who else can name a chapter 'Chicken Poo'? His sense of humour, balanced with some deep yet subtle messages, had me in tears. From his 'escape' to a public toilet, to what not to say to a celebrity, this is a Journal to entertain all readers."

"When I started reading this Journal I had a garden with a lawn and a patio. Now I have a vegetable patch, blisters, an aching back, and the biggest smile of my life. Thank you Fennel!"

From The Lighter Side:

"If self-actualisation is the pinnacle of one's development, then it can't be achieved if your mountain has two peaks...Being the 'best version' of yourself implies that you have other versions kept locked in a closet. Don't have any 'versions'. Just have one true, beautiful and pure form of you.
So climb your mountain, open your arms to the Creator who greets you there, and sing loudly to the world that stretches out beneath you. Write your name permanently on the landscape of your mind. Remember: you are a child of Nature. And you are free."

NO. 10

THE LIGHTER SIDE

There's a delicate balance between something meaning a great deal and that same thing becoming so serious that it's ludicrous. (Ever got stressed about what clothes to wear for an interview?) That's why *The Lighter Side* provides the encouragement, humour, anecdotes, reflections and honesty that are essential to Fennel's message of 'Stop – Unplug – Escape – Enjoy'. After all, we can only 'Enjoy' if we know how to smile when we get there.

READER TESTIMONIALS

"The Lighter Side was more than I expected. The deeper meaning within it – and the devastating honesty it conveys – made me question exactly where I am in my own life and what I can do to improve it for my family and me in the time that remains. Thank you Fennel for opening my eyes and adjusting my course."

"The opening chapter is the most startling, erudite, compassionate and open piece of writing I have ever read...thank you Fennel for sharing so much. It did and does mean a great deal."

From Friendship:

"What I'm talking about is proper friendship. The sort that is authentic, genuine and real. Where we can look into the eyes of another person and know what they're thinking. ...Because, as friends, we remember 'why' as much as 'when' or 'what'. Through good times and bad, we were there. Together. That's the bond, the unquestionable obligation that's freely given. It's the tightest hug, the biggest kiss, the tearful hello and the widest smile. If that's what it means to be a friend, or an extrovert, or just someone who cares for others then that's me to the last beat of my heart."

NO. 11

FRIENDSHIP

Written by the Friends of the Priory, with bonus chapters from Fennel, *Friendship* provides insights into what it means to be friends, how shared interests and beliefs support collective purpose, and how, when we're together, we can achieve more, appreciate more, and have more fun. It's about the broader world of Fennel's Priory and how it exists in others. It's a book written 'for us by us', with friendship as the theme.

READER TESTIMONIALS

"Possibly the greatest gift that this Journal bestows is to let us know that we are not alone."

"Like friendship itself, this Journal brings together people and meaning. It reminds us that 'together we are strong'. Thank you Fennel for leading our charge."

"The message (and evolution) of Fennel's Journal is most evident in this Friendship edition. With such obvious themes as identity and legacy, it's clear that what Fennel has shared over the years is a route-map to freedom and a stronger sense of self."

From Nature Escape:

"I am once again seeking an escape, to where I hope to find freedom and connect with the young man who handed me his trust ten years ago. This will be a faithful interpretation of the Priory, a fitting way to mark ten years of writing. As I said at the end of last year's Journal, 'One's journey through life is not linear; it's circular.' So let's go back to the beginning, and rediscover the quiet world."

NO. 12

NATURE ESCAPE

Nature Escape provides the most detailed account of a day that follows the motto of 'Stop – Unplug – Escape – Enjoy'. In it Fennel returns to the woodland of his youth to study its wildlife and savour its peacefulness.

Written in real-time, with twenty-four chapters that each represent an hour, the Journal is an account of how time spent outdoors in wild places enables us to observe the nature that's around us *and* within us.

READER TESTIMONIALS

"Fennel's Journal has always provided us with an escape, but now we know where the escape can lead. As promised, it leads to enjoyment – and very enjoyable it is too!"

"24 hours alone in a wood, with only 'the wild' for company? With Fennel as our guide, there's no such thing as 'alone'; only the warmth of knowing that quiet times are the fine times."

"By studying the nature within us and around us, Fennel demonstrates how to be 'at one' with nature."

From Book of Secrets:

"There's a greater man than me who can sum up our journey, a mountaineer who in 1865 first climbed the Matterhorn. Edward Whymper, over to you: 'There have been joys too great to be described in words, and there have been griefs upon which I have not dared to dwell, and with these in mind I say, climb if you will, but remember that courage and strength are naught without prudence, and that a momentary negligence may destroy the happiness of a lifetime. Do nothing in haste, look well to each step, and from the beginning think what may be the end.'"

NO. 13

BOOK OF SECRETS

Book of Secrets links all editions of Fennel's Journal together. With 14 Journals in the series, and 14 core chapters in this book, it's the 'one book to bind them all' with each chapter providing the continuity story from one Journal to the next.

Containing Fennel's previously private writing, it provides deep insight into the Fennel's Journal story. If you've ever wondered why each Journal is themed the way it is, or tried to find the metaphor in each edition, then *Book of Secrets* is for you.

READER TESTIMONIALS

"What a privilege: being able to read the private writing of my favourite author. Book of Secrets is a treat."

"Such honesty and wit. Fennel puts into words what I have only ever thought, or dare not say."

"Fennel's Journal really is a series – it's meant to be read as a whole. And now we have the key to unlock it."

From The Pursuit of Life:

"We can hide, or we can strive – for a life of our making. With endless possibilities and opportunities to reach for our dreams, we owe it to ourselves to dream big and keep going, irrespective of what we might encounter. Sadly, the thing that most limits our success is not others, but ourselves. How strongly we believe, how confidently we act, how fiercely we react, how passionately we want, and how life-affirmingly compelled we are to grow and blossom; that's how we keep going, no matter what, to be the person we want to be, living the life we deserve, in dreams that are real."

NO. 14

THE PURSUIT OF LIFE

The Pursuit of Life concludes the Fennel's Journal story. It's a reflective tome that provides Fennel's commentary on the journey and a 'behind the scenes' view of the challenges and rewards of a life rebuilt on one's terms.

It's an account of how the series came to be and how it evolved, and includes much of Fennel's private writing, several of the original handwritten drafts, correspondence between The Friends, and encouragement for those on similar paths. Ultimately it shows how the Fennel's Journal series can be used as a route map to a more fulfilling life.

READER TESTIMONIALS

"A life retold, for our benefit. Fennel is to be congratulated for everything he's achieved – on paper and in life."

"It's his life in the books, but it could so very easily be ours. Fennel has a way of seeing truth in the severe and the sublime, and bringing it home."

"Can this really be the end? When dreams are real, we never wake from them. More books Fennel, please!"

www.ingramcontent.com/pod-product-compliance
Lightning Source LLC
Chambersburg PA
CBHW030331230426
43661CB00032B/1372/J